JOSEPH

THE RING OF THE NIBELUNG

The Case of Richard Wagner

The Art of Freedom and Interpretation in the Middle of the Twentieth Century

Original translation from the German completely revised by Pierre Watter
Editors: Stanley Trevor, Pierre Watter

anarcho press

First Published:

Contemporary Issues, Vol. 5, No 19, August - September, 1954.

Revised, re-translated, and reset in this Edition, January 2000

© Pierre Watter)
   Stanley Trevor)   December 1999

Published by:

Anarcho Press, 7 Portland Terrace, Nairn, Nairnshire
Scotland IV12 4AS .   Tel: 01667 452476

ISBN No: 0 906469 24 4

Distributed by:

Central Books, 99Wallis Road, London E9 5LN.
                             Tel: 0181 966 4854

Single copies available from publishers

Printed by Intype London Ltd. Units 3/4 Elm Grove Industrial Estate, Elm Grove, Wimbledon SW19 4HE.   Tel: 020 8947 7863

Joseph Weber, 1909 - 1951

About the Author

Joseph Weber (1901 - 1959) belongs to the less known exiles from the circle of socialist groups of the twenties and thirties. He studied music and philosophy and when still young became involved with the radical left. He was forced to flee from Hitler's Germany, was interned in France, and emigrated to the USA in 1940, where he pioneered the internationally active groups, including in Germany itself, Great Britain, America, and South Africa, ranged around the publications 'Dinge der Zeit' (German language) and 'Contemporary Issues' (English language) - ["of which I was an avid reader" *Noam Chomsky*]. An expert only in the field of music, he yet made major contributions to philosophy in its true sense as the science of the sciences, in its applications to contemporary conditions in the fields of politics, consciousness, and culture and functioned as an early and devastating critic of Stalinism (and its sub-branches, Trotskyism and Mao-ism, etc.) as well as American imperialism. Shortly before his death, he returned to Germany where he became a committed fighter against the re-armament of Germany in the early fifties. His early death was an irreplaceable loss.

Editorial Note

The Ring of the Nibelung was first published in the German magazine "Dinge der Zeit" at the end of 1947.

Now, some fifty-five years later, coincidentally with the 60th anniversary of the declaration of war on Germany in 1939, there has been a tremendous resurgence of interest in the history of the rise and practice of Nazism, accompanied by repetition of the myths regarding the responsibility of the German people for this phenomenon, as well as a plenitude of apologists for Hitler even among 'respectable' academics and professors of history as exemplified in such BBC programmes as 'The Wrong War', where Hitler, at least up to the invasion of Czechoslovakia, was presented as the saviour of the German people, as well as the recent programme under the title of "Hitler's Willing Partners"; also in the programme devoted to Richard Wagner in the BBC series under the rubric ' The Great Composers' accompanied by the presentation of Richard Wagner as Nazism's prescient embodiment. Even in the new millennium, a recent programme featuring cartoons made by English cartoonists about the Germans during the first world war (1914-1918), presenting obscenities such as images of big fat animal-like Germans in military uniforms killing and eating babies, had as their background Siegfried's funeral march from the Goetterdaemerung. Joseph Weber's assertion, therefore, that his study 'has lost none of its topicality' would appear to be well proved.

The entry of T.W.Adorno, one of the most outstanding philosophical thinkers and writers of the day and, with Horkheimer and Marcuse, one of the founders of the prestigious Frankfurt Institute for Social Research, on the 'anti-

Wagner' front was a significant ideological event, one which Joseph Weber felt could not pass unremarked. The following polemic against the Adorno piece constituted his reply, endorsement of which was given by Marcuse himself.

What Joseph Weber refers to as 'the campaign for the 'collective guilt' of the Axis peoples, (with preference given to Germany)' for the atrocities of Nazism seems to have lost none of its fury. Especially relevant might be the Publication of Daniel Goldhagen's *Hitler's Willing Executioners; Ordinary Germans and the Holocaust*, which achieved the status of a best seller 50 years after the events to which it referred took place. The reader's attention is also drawn to the publication of an excellent rebuttal of this piece written by Jack Suhl and published in the magazine *Outlook*, October/November 1996/7.

One thing that these programmes have in common is little or no reference at all to the fact that the Nazi regime was a rule of terror. The price for opposition was - the concentration camp,[1] but there is no mention of the fact that the institution of the concentration camp was a uniquely *British* invention (given to the world during the Boer War) in which over 120,000 Africans and 20,000 Boer women and children perished. No doubt the British officers on the Transvaal veldt spent their evenings listening to and reading Wagner.

The real fact is that the so-called mass demonstrations so lovingly presented as 'proof' were stage managed. People were bundled out of their homes and offices and forced onto the streets. An acquaintance who was on the streets at such a

---

1. These were presented in the programme as the solution to the problem of the economy 'overheating' - where *have* we heard that phrase before?

'popular' demonstration and standing in silence told me that he suddenly felt a knife at his throat with the question hissed in his ear: "Lost your voice, have you?" As the list of daily arrests were read out, any reaction stronger than a raised eyebrow would result in that person being immediately led away. Neighbours did not even dare to look at each other.

The only mass emotion experienced by the German people was fear. Parents dared not speak in front of their neighbours or even their children for fear being reported or an indiscretion on their children's part which could lead to their arrest. No homage at all was paid to the countless heroes who went to their deaths in the resistance against Hitler. One wonders how many of those safely pontificating from their armchairs sixty years later about the responsibility of the German people would have exhibited comparable courage.

It is a matter of history that all opposition was mercilessly stamped out and the inmates of concentration and slave labour camps were by no means confined to Jews.. Nor was anything of this mentioned in the programme.

On the contrary, the subliminal attempt to root these phenomena in the 'German Psyche' also has its place in the presentation of the BBC. The film footage of the SS troops cavorting on their horses and playing at hunting in the English style, for which they had a high regard, presented them showing off their horsemanship to the accompaniment of a Mozart Horn concerto, not withstanding the fact that Mozart was Austrian..

Even the persecution of the Jews merited no more than a three minute reference.

On the other hand, it is indeed now possible to refer to a

phenomenon known as the 'holocaust industry'; its aim, the defense of Israel against any criticism and the appropriation of the Shoah in exclusivity for this purpose. The Holocaust Industry has steadfastly refused to give any mention to the extermination of the Gypsies on the various holocaust memorials in Washington etc. And now in Berlin. The Gypsies had a fate exactly parallel to that of the Jews. But their mention at the memorials would detract from the Jewish uniqueness, from exploiting the killings for the Jewish State, absolving any criticism of the Israeli State's appalling treatment of the Palestinians under the rubric of 'antisemitism'. A letter to the Guardian (28/1/2000) succinctly pinpoints the situation:

> "No decent person would deny the Jews proper commemoration for the Holocaust. What opponents object to is its use as a symbol of Jewish victimhood and thus as a justification for Israeli aggression and oppression.
>
> If Jews and Israelis want to heal the wounds of their past let them strive to properly commemorate the 1948 massacre of the Palestinian village of Deir Yassin which, along with other coercions, signaled the dispossession and exile of the Palestinian people." *Paul Elson*

As Guenter Grass, Nobel Prize winner, has stated: a new "selection" is taking place. Those who are selected to survive are the Jews, and the memory of the others, the Gypsies, homosexuals, Jehovah's Witnesses, political and religious opponents, etc, who also perished are sent to oblivion.

For all this, including the holocaust itself, Wagner is to be presented as progenitor.

Apart from the BBC programmes mentioned above, a five

minute trawl on the Internet under the rubric 'Wagner and the Nazis' revealed the following amongst hundreds of entries selected at random, dated '© 1998'. and un-attributed. Under the title *"Black Dahlia and the Aryan Ideal"*. and subtitled 'Racial Purity and the Aryan Ideal' we read:

> "The racial purity ideas of the Third Reich have their foundations in the ideas of three influential people: a French writer, an English author. and a German composer. These creative individuals shaped the doctrines of Adolf Hitler and fashioned vague but powerful ideas of racial inequality and hatred......finally, one of the greatest influences to (sic!) Hitler was the German composer Richard Wagner......According to Wagner [the] German "hero-spirit" was a element of pure Nordic-Aryan blood and the untainted Germans should take any measures necessary to keep the Aryan race free of inferiority....."

The innate falsity of this statement is precisely what is exposed in Weber's study, but what is involved was set out by Noam Chomsky[2]:

> "A principle familiar to propagandists is that the doctrines to be instilled in the target audience should not be articulated; that would only expose them to reflection, enquiry, and very likely, ridicule. The proper procedure is to drill them home by constantly presupposing them so that they become the very condition of discourse."

It would therefore seem that Joseph Weber's assertion that "in the delay in its publication, [the piece] has lost none of its topicality in three and a half years" could be extended to fifty

---

2. Letters from Lexington - Reflections on Propaganda (published AK press, Edinburgh) in a letter dated 15thn April 1990.

five odd years without any loss of verisimilitude.

The monumental genius that was Richard Wagner, creator of the miraculous introduction to The Rheingold, will not leave the stage of history and his enrolment in the neo-Nazi cause can be understood as the attempt to use his prestige, authority, and standing to lend this virulent growth ideological credibility. This must by all means be resisted. In this lies the *raison d'être* for the re-publication of this essay.

Stanley Trevor
January, 2000

Preliminary Note 1947

"The Ring of the Nibelung " bears the date 1944. It thus appears after a long delay but has, in my opinion, lost none of its topicality in three and a half years. It is important for the reader to keep the above date in mind inasmuch as he will find occasion, now and then, to orientate himself by it. So, for instance, when it is said that "already" the races of the world are swinging back over Channel and Ocean to the Rhine to win the ring of accursed gold for themselves - this is a remark aimed at the landing of the Allied forces on the French coast then directly impending. In the same way, the "prediction" that, after "Siegfried's" dispatch, the "scuffle over the possession of the world dominating ring would not be long in coming" is to be considered under the date given. This prediction has been confirmed up to the hilt, and makes the world still more intimately familiar than before with "the intervention of the blind will". I am, however, not "proud" of it: it belongs, if only for myself and my friends, in the category of the obvious.

In a general way, the date shows further that we do not belong to those who have only belatedly opened their only too often, and only too willingly, closed eyes. At that time, the campaign for the "collective guilt" of the Axis peoples (with preference given to Germany) neared the peak of its fury - the preparation of public opinion for what was to follow with the Morgenthau Plan and Potsdam was in full swing. With the end of the war in Europe, an opposition to the "collective guilt" thesis gradually formed itself and much water was poured into the once richly flowing wine also by some previous advocates. Now and again, one even finds articles which object to the "psychological nonsense" connected with the guilt question - of course, without apprehending the *ideological* significance appertaining to psychology as such in the concept of "collective guilt". A great deal will yet have to be said about this opposition and its literature, but, as far as I can see, it moves entirely on the level of "making allowances", i.e. it points out that there were "many German anti-fascists", that the history of all great nations abounds in wars and crimes, that the "democracies" promoted Hitler, etc. All that is correct and useful, but insufficient. This study seeks to pose the real problem and, by its solution, also to give political impulses.

1

Posing of the Question

The "Ring of the Nibelung" has little to do with Richard Wagner and much to do with the intellectual conditions of our time. Wagner's music plays no part at all in it. The word "Ring" serves only as a symbol of the smothering economic, political and ideological system of compulsion which envelops present day society. What this system is about will automatically be brought out in the course of the investigation when we encounter the connections of the poetry and philosophy of Richard Wagner with the problems of our time. First a glance must be thrown at certain contemporary conditions and the reasons which provoke special reflections of the "Ring of the Nibelung".

Our time, in consequence of an economic, political and cultural disintegration which has been going on for decades, is distinguished on the one hand by the grossest ignorance, and, on the other, by the grossest arrogance based on fragmentary and sham knowledge. It stands in philosophical, intellectual. and political-moral respects on an incomparably low level. Nothing is any longer tackled from the ground up and given time to mature. Instead, the merest superficial glance at anything suffices for its dismissal with an impertinently "assured" judgement. Critique thus sees itself hindered on all sides: it must "explain" at great length even the most simple and obvious things, because the average capacity for thinking has sunk to nothing and can be measured only by the extraordinarily "high standard" of co-existing arrogance. In view of the present conditions, one can understand the plaintive exclamation of Theodore Lessing: "Nothing has become so uncommon in the Western world as the instinctive capacity for clarity in matters of judgement."

Thus, for example, daily life brings us into contact with an abundant accumulation of legends, brought into the world by people with a special interest. These legends refer to the "basic corruption" of the Germans, the role of Germany as the "trouble maker of the world", the irremediable ideological infection of German youth, the responsibility of all Germans for the horrors of fascism. Statesmen, politicians, merchants, literati, scientists, newspaper publishers, reporters, poets, union leaders, associations, mere venal rabble.....together they form a phalanx which is ceaselessly active and leaves no hole unfulfilled in the vast edifice of legends. These professional manufacturers of legends aim especially at re-writing German history, the lives of great and minor Germans, etc. from top to bottom, They give everything a new meaning, "interpret" everything according to their purpose.

The finished model for such baseness has been supplied by Stalin and his school. Western "civilisation" seems to work in accordance with the prescription: "One must stupify consciousness and better the mammoth work of Stalinist falsification, calumny, and poisoning". However it be, there can be no doubt: Stalin's seed has been lavishly sown and sprouts.

Thus attention is focussed on Luther, Kant, Fichte, Hegel,

Lasalle, Nietzche, Marx. Engels, Schopenhauer, Wagner. They are all "precursors of Fascism"; or, if not, the least that can be said is that every known or unknown German is a sadist, a masochist, or both at once.

Here now, whoever takes a stand against the deception of the public will have the surprise of his life, in Lessing's sense. The realisation dawns upon him, the moment he begins to think, that everything is found natural and obvious, except what actually is so.

The Wagner legend may serve as an *ad hoc* example, and as a model for the rest. It is a monstrous legend; but as soon as one tackles it and seeks to counter the swindle, one has first of all to "justify" oneself. The greater the "educated" impertinence, the further away lies the instinctive feeling that natural things need no justification, or, more exactly, that the justification of a procedure lies always in itself, in its result.

One can, of course, acquire indispensable merit by taking issue with the result, i.e. by showing that it is defective or inferior, that it was obtained by an experiment with an unsuitable object, etc. One can, however, never ask how it comes about that Jacques Barzun brought out a book about "Darwin, Marx, and Wagner' or the unspeakable Emil Ludwig his autobiography under the title "Scribblifax of Breslau". Just where it is a matter of finding out what ends are pursued in a given case, just there the stupidity of the present-day "artful dodger" is capable of saying with great "obviousness": "Your ideas are quite correct.....but why did you pick this subject?"

The over-clever "but" has, of course, no other purpose than to hide the fact that the critic knows nothing about correct or incorrect ideas; however, one can always trip him up by means of his own objections. To castigate the ignorant arrogance which one meets with everywhere in public life is a peremptory requirement for public health. Each slap in the face is an act of revenge for the insults to natural propriety that demands that everyone should take the trouble of becoming acquainted with the *matter* before he or she joins in the discussion.

Of course there is, in the given circumstances, a "fatality" about impudence, lack of manners and ignorance which cannot be prevented from cropping up. However, one has to turn energetically against those for whom the recognition of the fatality of certain phenomena does not entail the recognition of the equal fatality of the fight against them. What exists today, even what has been so for a long time, need not remain so for ever. The outcome is decided by the struggle. To consider fatalism as "one-sided" was thought wrong even in Greek philosophy. For the Greek sages, maxim and anti-maxim came together. Nor was it beneath their dignity to give practical effect to the anti-maxim. Zeno, of whose doctrine fatalism was an integral part, took up the whip when he caught a slave stealing. The slave tried to entrap Zeno in his own doctrine, claiming that fate had predestined him to steal. "But" what thence followed for the Eleatic was only that the same fate had predestined the slave to be whipped for his act.

It is, therefore, not at all beneath one's so-called dignity to answer the overbearing critic: the present subject, or the case of Richard Wagner, has been selected because it yields very definite results, and those again in a very definite shape which would not have been got from another subject. You may declare yourself uninterested in subject and results, yet this is never an argument - it is no more than an instance of the diversity of human interests. The absurdity of what you are pleased to use as an argument becomes the more evident, the more unimportant becomes the point of departure one chooses, since one can get to the centre from any point. The difference lies only in that one has, from different starting points, always to break through different strata. The real task is the struggle against the egregious narrow-mindedness which, in its "perfection", takes itself to be the centre. When, therefore, arguments like these crop up, it will always be shown upon closer examination that nothing but impotence which shies from the effort of thinking, learning, moving, and, above all, from the *consequences,* lies behind them.

Amiable as dilettantism may be in the private sphere, be it in speaking, writing, philosophising, music-making etc., as damaging is it in its effects when driven into public life by commodity production. In the conditions brought about by commodity production, ignorance turns into conscious swindling. Swindling, with all its accompaniments arising from general competition (baseness of character, misinterpretation, calumny, falsification, unscrupulousness, vulgarity, unwillingness to call things by their proper names and to describe them with exactitude) immediately becomes the supreme law. With the spread of competition, the instincts unleashed by it produce the direct opposite of what the vulgar mind expects. They do not produce higher development and "refinement", but instead produce mediocrity on a mass scale, the manufacture of trash and sham, together with pompous ignorance which rules by sheer quantity.

It is the same process as can be seen with "white" bread which has become a mass product on the basis of industrial farming and baking. From the point of view of nutrition, this product of industrial competition is worthless and even harmful. By means of ever finer milling, all nourishing substances are eliminated from the cereals, until at last only the "white" remains, the "pure" starch, the quantitative worthlessness. In this way, commodity production achieves, in the first place, the paradox of making higher profits with inferior goods (which, of course, taste as sweet as Heine's *"Nonnenfürzchen "*[3]) than it would with superior ones; secondly, human beings ruin their physical and spiritual lives in the belief that they are nursing their health and finally, moreover, the working masses are obliged to pay for their ruin in ready money, the getting of which demands from them unceasing sacrifice of health and happiness.

Marx made the pertinent observation:

> "In bourgeois society the "legal fiction" prevails that every person, as buyer of commodities, has an encyclopaedic knowledge of them."[4]

In practice, this statement amounts to the following: if people knew *what* in fact is bought and sold, and how they are made to have artificial needs which anyone who knew all about commodities would not have, the bulk of commodities would become unsaleable, and bourgeois society would immediately fall to bits. The same holds for the overwhelming majority of "spiritual" commodities. If people knew with what they are irremediably and continually poisoned, bourgeois society could not exist an hour longer. Everything rests upon the juridical fiction that every individual has a universal knowledge of commodities, something immediately supplemented by the fiction that each individual is *per se* an encyclopaedia, a matchless treasure of knowledge and wisdom. Hence, the more

---

3. *Nonnenfürszchen* are little cakes. Coincidentally, *Nonnen* are nuns, *Fürzchen* is the diminutive of *Fürz* (fart).

4. Karl Marx. *Das Kapital*, Chapter 1.

the spiritually disinherited readers of present newspapers and magazines fancy themselves as knowing everything (a deliberately cultivated delusion), the more defencelessly are they delivered into the hands of their tormentors.

To return to the matter under investigation: The question: "Why, precisely, have you selected old Wagner of all subjects?" appears not merely thoughtless and pompous but simply silly. For, while in the case of the autobiography of Scribblifax of Breslau we have, after all, only to do with scrap production, Wagner rules the field now as before on the opera stage, in concerts and discussion, to say nothing of his great influence on musical composition. One may dislike Wagner's domination and influence, but dislike is not enough to dismiss as "old Wagner", a phenomenon so alive and overwhelming in its vitality. The critic may of course avoid the effort required for a thorough study of Wagner, Nietzche, Hegel etc.. He may, moreover, have his private prejudices, may not want to read, to listen, to exert himself. But then he must remain silent and forgo taking part in a public discussion of things which have nothing to do with him.

Proceeding thus, the posing of the question concludes with a particularly precise answer for children and old dogs: dealing with the critic's objections and with present day conditions prepares us for the case of Wagner, as the overture does for the opera. Is it really necessary to add that the general (the manufacture of legends on the grounds of vested interests) is reflected in the particular (the case of Wagner) and the particular in the general. But be that as it may - the curtain rises for the introduction of the characters.

2

Posing of the Question in the Light of a Concrete Example

The *Journal for Social Research* published a study by T.W.Adorno entitled "Fragments about Wagner" *(No. 1/2, Vol.8, Librairie Fèlix Alcan, Paris)*. True to the conviction that the result is what justifies the undertaking, the question is naturally *not* "Why did Adorno choose Wagner 'at all' as his theme?" One could only assert the reverse: Let us see *why* he came to write about Wagner and what he brings to light.

Like everything else so far presented by the members of The Institute for Social Research, Adorno's study stood on a high technical level. It assumed, as if it were the most natural thing in the world, an acquaintance on the reader's part with an array of philosophical questions, with systems of philosophy, with poets, with artistic, historical, and technical problems in music, etc. etc. without knowledge of which the study cannot be fully understood, still less critically examined and weighed. This stated, it must be said at once, in view of the backwardness and indolence that characterise our era, everyone, including T.W.Adorno, has the right to assume, as Feuerbach put it, "spirit also in the reader", i.e. knowledge. The conditions in which we live are, for the most part, not created by ourselves. In particular, the regrettable split of society into a small band of "specialists" on the one hand, and the mass of the ignorant on the other, is a result of the social division of labour that simply cannot be done away with by complaints.

It matters little what attitude private persons, political parties, groups espousing particular interests, etc., adopt *vis-à-vis* the products of specialists. The fact, however, that these specialists lead society by the nose in every sphere of social activity, and that they themselves work exclusively according to the laws of competition, means that the whole of society remains in "spiritual" respects as well the slave of the most universal and vulgar competition. As in the economic and political spheres, so even in the "most august" spheres of philosophy, science, art etc.. Only a few know whether they are served useful results or sham production, error, charlatanry, and outright fraud. General competition is, incidentally, the reason why, on the one hand, so many artistic, scientific, philosophical, religious and political tendencies exist, and why, on the other, they so furiously fight one another, go bankrupt, unite with and against one another, as is the case in the life of states, industries, commercial firms, insurance companies and small shopkeepers. Obviously, competition produces, besides cheap and trash, also grandiose progress. Such progress, however, is used in the same way as the discovery of dynamite, or the conquest of the air by aviation. They become weapons with which one extends competition and beats down the opponent.

There is therefore only one way of destroying the tyranny of specialists; one must beat them with their own weapons, i.e. make specialisation a general phenomenon by multiplying the number of specialists and thereby abolish it as a particular class.[5]

---

5. Parties bent upon 'changing the world' that renounce themselves becoming specialists in all fields and destroying competition in the general interest doom themselves from the beginning to the frightful provincialism of small shopkeepers fighting one another that characterizes present day 'revolutionary' organizations without exception. If ever one of these organizations came to power in its present condition, it would be bound to lose it again simply because of being completely at the mercy of specialists who would lead it to certain catastrophe. This does not apply to the followers of Stalin who are nothing but paid swindlers and have tasks other than the advancement of mankind. It has also nothing to do with the

The greater the number of people who have sufficient knowledge to bring to heel the tyrants in control of their education and opinions, the more the professional specialist disappears and makes room for the really educated human being. Thus the obvious thing consists in taking things as they are and trying to cope with them.

In the case of Adorno, it soon became apparent that he too (despite the high technological level) was one of the manufacturers of legends and was filled with a strange petty hatred of his subject. This hatred, again, would have been a quite unproblematical matter, a phenomenon needing no explanation, had it enabled Adorno to "finish off" the real Wagner and his work in a strictly objective fashion. Instead of that, there spoke a man who, while pretending to "hate" the "existing world" had made himself one with it, and now furiously attacked the "mischief-maker" Wagner (something that remains to be proved). To do so, he used a means favoured and employed by apologists for the *status quo*, calling upon the science of psychology to be his hand-maiden.

The fruits of modern psychology will manifest themselves at the proper time. Here it suffices to note that our noble 'science' prepares legends specifically for the circle of its victims who lack the capacity for checking them, legends that present-day society urgently needs in order to veil its true character. In the end it supplies nothing different from what is produced, on the appropriate low level and for daily business, by creatures such as an Emil Ludwig. It would indeed be a grave mistake to

---

disconsolate creations calling themselves Social-Democratic parties; but rather with those organizations that, abstractly considered, have better foundations, but go about their tasks in an absurdly limited fashion.

suppose that science has nothing to do with the demagogic exigencies of the day. In reality, a significant quantum of specialists is busy preserving illusions about bourgeois society. It is only once these illusions have become entrenched in all spheres and have been adequately buttressed that the coarse Emil Ludwig's of this world hope to succeed in their work of falsification. The popular prejudice is built up after the pattern: If even 'pure' science gravely shakes its head, there must be something in the rantings of the, in many respects, unpleasant Mr Emil Ludwig, for all that he often 'exaggerates'.

The use and abuse of psychology had already been commented on by Hegel, and his remarks appear particularly pertinent to the matter in hand:

> "What is called the 'pragmatic' writing of history has in modern times frequently sinned in its treatment of great historical characters and defaced and tarnished the true conception of them by [the] fallacious separation of the outward from the inward. Not content with telling the unvarnished tale of the great acts which have been wrought by the heroes of the world's history and with acknowledging that their inward being corresponds with the import of their acts, the pragmatic historian fancies himself justified and even obliged to trace the supposed secret motives that lie behind the open facts of the record. The historian, in that case, is supposed to write with more depth in proportion as he succeeds in tearing away the aureole from all that has been heretofore held grand and glorious, and in depressing it, so far as its origin and proper significance are concerned, to the level of vulgar mediocrity. To make these pragmatical researches in history easier, it is usual to recommend the study of psychology, which is supposed to make us acquainted with the real motives of human actions. The psychology in question, however, is only that petty knowledge of men which looks away from the essential and permanent in

human nature to fasten its glance on the casual and private features shown in isolated instincts and passions.

> A pragmatical psychology ought at least to leave the historian, who investigates the motives at the ground of great actions, a choice between the 'substantial' interests of patriotism, justice, religious truth and the like, on the one hand, and the subjective and 'formal' vanity, ambition, avarice, and the like, on the other. The latter are, however, the motives which must be viewed by the pragmatists as really efficient, otherwise the assumption of a contrast between inward (the disposition of the agent) and the outward (the import of the act) would fall to the ground. But inward and outward have in truth the same content....If the heroes of history had been actuated by subjective and formal interests alone, they would never have accomplished what they have. And if we have due regard to the unity between the inner and the outer, we must own that great men willed what they did, and did what they willed "[6]

This will serve immediately to plunge us into *medias res*.

3.

Details of T.W.Adorno's Presentation

The peculiar colouring T.W.Adorno gives to everything that has to do with Wagner recoils on Adorno from the start. For example:

> "'Rienzi' not only became Wagner's first big success that brought him fame and position; it still noisily fills opera houses, although the Meyerbeerian conception of grand opera

---

6. Hegel: *The Doctrine of Essence,* from the Encyclopedia of the Philosophical Sciences, translated by W. Wallace.

Germanism and where it led him. Wagner was not the first, nor would he be the last, artist to be overwhelmed by his material and to have found more in it than he expected. The 'glorification of Germanism' is only the first reproach to be levelled at him and may thus serve as a starting point.

Whoever aspires to be something other than an ignorant babbler, a dilettante ruled by his emotions, a conscienceless demagogue, or simply a fraud, will first of all look for solid foundations and ask himself: "How do things stand?"

The mere posing of this question leads to the re-establishment of historical truth, a category which has now become almost completely outmoded and which, in the moral sphere, is called elementary justice. A fascist can concoct as many lies as he wishes - a substantive democrat, on the other hand, who transgresses in this sphere and violates the most elementary principles of real democracy, must be labelled either an idiot or a scoundrel. Taking for granted, for the present, as given Wagner's nationalism, glorification of Germanism etc., matters nevertheless stand as follows:

One cannot reproach Wagner, who, as a participant in the Dresden uprising, and 'as one who returned to grace', was a *bourgeois*, for having been a bourgeois. Just as little can one reproach *any* bourgeois for nationalistic fervour and glorifying his or her own people 'as such'. National pride, even chauvinistic arrogance and exclusiveness, are characteristics which belong 'naturally' to the inhabitants of young national states. Countless bourgeois of any given country share these with countless goes against Wagner's own norms of the music-drama as completely as does the "Novice of Palermo". The opening scene, to be sure, no longer glorifies free sensuality. It denounces it. A gang of young noblemen are on the point of an assault on the virtue of the chaste Irene. She is the blindly devoted sister of Rienzi, the last Roman tribune, and the first bourgeois terrorist."

To characterise Adorno's method: The Meyerbeerian conception of grand opera which, in Rienzi, goes against Wagner's own norms of the music-drama, is a defamatory flourish without sense and content. People may enjoy themselves as much at grand opera, German song-play, chamber opera, music-drama, etc., but what has that to do with Wagner's later "norms"? The only thing one can say with some degree of sense needs no "although"; all it needs is the statement that Wagner went on developing, gave up grand opera, and devoted himself to the "drama of the future".

This unimportant flourish must be chalked up against Adorno because it follows immediately upon the statement, equally defamatory in intent and factually indefensible that 'Rienzi' today still noisily fills opera "houses". Anyone can, by referring to opera house programmes, easily discern that performances of 'Rienzi' (the last of the tribunes and Adorno's first conveyor belt) are about as frequent as two-headed cows.

It can be seen that Adorno, right from the start, is eager to suggest that Wagner was, allegedly, a keen supporter of "bourgeois terror" and terrorists, and that this attitude was warmly supported by the public. He makes not the slightest effort to explain that, notwithstanding certain similarities between present day dictatorships and early bourgeois terrorists, there are at the same time very great differences. The political pacemakers of the bourgeoisie, be they Luther, Calvin, Cromwell, Danton, Robespierre, Napoleon, Louis Napoleon and so on, have at all times been dictators and terrorists. A learned man like Adorno ought to know that it is pure demagogy that amounts to underpinning the present day need for lies, if, in a historical investigation, one does not make plain the way in which one revolutionary dictatorship, e.g. Cromwell's, differs from the counter-revolutionary dictatorship and terrorism of a Hitler. Historically it is precisely "Rienzi" that can be interpreted only on the basis of the conditions characterising Germany on the eve of its *positively* orientated and unconditionally progressive *bourgeois* revolution.

Here generalisation might have been made directly opposed to the demagogy of Adorno. Thus he might have used the example of Rienzi to repeat what Marx might have said about the bourgeois revolutionary minded Wagner:

> "Men make their own history, but they do not make it just as they please; they do not make it under circumstances chosen by themselves, but under circumstances directly encountered, given, and transmitted from the past. The tradition of all the dead generations weighs like a nightmare on the brain of the living. And just when they seem engaged in revolutionising themselves and things, in creating something that as never yet existed, precisely in such periods of revolutionary crisis they anxiously conjure up the spirits of the past to their service and borrow from them names, battle-cries and costumes in order to present the new scene of world history in this time honoured disguise and this borrowed language. Thus Luther donned the mask of the Apostle Paul, the revolution of 1789 to 1814 draped itself alternately as the Roman republic and the Roman empire, and the revolution of 1848 knew nothing better than to parody, now 1789, now the revolutionary tradition of 1793 to

1795."[7]

Wagner, too, borrowed names, slogans and costumes of the past in order to give expression to his revolutionary moods and ideas concerning art and politics. And therein lies the reason why he could not escape the general laws of the bourgeois revolution as a *minority revolution.*

The law of all revolutions in which one ruling minority is removed and replaced by another ruling minority, consists in its appearing as a "peoples revolution". "Fully conscious" of its historic mission, the minority comes forward in the name of general aims and as the representatives of the people. To give the movement of the minority the appearance of a majority movement it already suffices that the mass of the people take a passive attitude towards it. Most minority revolutions are, however, distinguished by the fact that they have the support of the masses and bring to power a more radical wing which pushes the revolution sufficiently forward. When this wing, with its "dictator", like Robespierre or Rienzi, has sufficiently secured the historically necessary changes in an exaggerated form, then it usually loses it own head, that is, is removed and disappears, together with its exaggerations, in the abyss of history.

On such sound social foundations, the investigations and critical writings of the Institute for Social Research might have begun with some hope for a good result. It might perhaps have compared the character of Rienzi's Roman uprising directed against the then "libertine" style of life, with the dictatorship of the virtuous Robespierre, and might have discovered why both terrorists, apart from their shared "asceticism", also have in

---

7. Karl Marx, *The Eighteenth Brumaire of Louis Bonaparte, Part I.*

common a leaning towards solemn arrangements or towards "cult". It could, in certain conditions, have been correctly said that Wagner had "an inkling of the fickleness of bourgeois terror, of the forlornness of self-appointed heroism." In which case one would have to admire the penetration with which Wagner represented Rienzi, in essence just like Napoleon, who took the crown of Caesar out of the hands of the Pope and himself placed it on his own head, only to be buried under the ruins of his own magnificence. It would then really have been possible to find out why Wagner had to leave grand opera to Meyerbeer, Halévy, Gounod, etc., had to develop away from it and treat it with hatred and contempt.

For Germany was not so lucky as France. It entered bourgeois development as the famous late-comer. In its miserable bourgeois revolution, the coming catastrophe of all society had already announced itself. Wagner's genius saw in this the end of individual tragedy and strove towards the drama of society. Wagner's "Gesamtkunstwerk" is the attempt to reflect the collective drama of society. If, as a work of art, it therefore shares the problematic character of that society, the secret of its attractive power is, nonetheless, it universality.

Adorno's social research, however, sets no store by tracing the interconnections which have become visible today. Instead it produces the connections with the rabble who see a prelude to Hitler in everything that has lived and all that has happened in Germany, always excepting, of course, the case of the individual speaking or writing in that strain.[8] Adorno does not consider for

---

8. At this point I shall eliminate an objection which takes the form of "why deal with Adorno whose treatise is already several years old and known only to a very narrow circle?" This objection reveals once more the thoughtless self-defence that would like to talk the fact that Adorno's

a second that the rise of society is something different from its decline. Still less does he consider that all bourgeois revolutions are pregnant to bursting point with "people's community", freedom, equality, fraternity, and similar phrases. Unconcernedly, he leaves aside everything historical and once more angrily attacks just what is obvious. In the style of the gossip columnist, he charges Rienzi with the proclamation of a "peoples' community", common to all bourgeois revolutions, and fires away:

> "In this peoples' community, the subjugated are taken in only titularly [as if this were not the case in every bourgeois revolution and code of law. *J.W.*] 'Now I shall make Rome great

---

method and argumentation are *typical* and are used in numerous schools of which not the least is the Institute for Social Research itself, off the earth. The task is quite simply to unmask this method and manner of argumentation and to hit at the "pure" science without which the rabble could not exist. It may at this point (May 1953) be added that an enlarged edition (in book form) of Adorno's *Fragments* has appeared in Germany under the title "Versuch über Wagner" (Suhrkampf Verlag 1952). In a note to his book, Adorno declares that his:

> "Fragments on Wagner" had their modest fate: an extensive polemic appeared in "Dinge der Zeit", London. It only came into the hands of the author after years, when it was far too late for a reply. Still, he believed that the text of the chapters already printed should 'essentially' remain the same."

Well, the author of the Ring knows for sure that already in 1948 at least one *prominent* member of the Institute for Social Research had *read* and *approved* the Ring. But what is more important: why should it be too late for a *reply* when it is not too late to publish the *attacked text*. Adorno's statement reads rather like an "objectively" masqueraded attempt to evade a controversy in which many are interested for the sake of knowledge, truth, and - justice. "Dinge der Zeit" will publish any answer Adorno wants to write, but will treat with disdain excuses that are none.

and free. I shall rouse it from its slumber, and those whom you see in the dust, I shall make free citizens of Rome' As the "hero of peace" gives the feudalists to understand that he does not intend to do them any serious harm, so he limits the claims of the subjugated merely to their consciousness. '...by helping the base, raising those reduced to nothing, you have turned the people's shame to greatness, fame and majesty....'"

Seen historically or as 'social research' and not psychologically and morally, this is just what had to be done, in no matter what guise, by the bourgeoisie in Wagner's time.

To use a simile: the charge cannot be levied against people who, at a time when the child was still growing in the mother's womb, declared that mother and child formed an organic 'community'. The deception about the antagonism between mother and child, which later fully develops, and the conscious fraud, begin only when the child has attained independence of the mother and the quacks are trying to push it back into the womb.

Thus it was not Wagner who found himself in the role of the swindling proponents of people's community, but those who betrayed the subjugated to the bourgeoisie at the moment of their full independence, a betrayal all the more horrible and base since it was committed not in the name of bourgeois 'freedom', but in that of the subjugated themselves.

The *real* precursors of Hitler are not therefore to be found among the midwives of bourgeois society, but among those who delivered the subjugated defencelessly to Hitler. These were, in the first place, the "communists" and the Social Democrats. The "communists" carried on their business of mass murder on Stalin's orders, the bloodiest, most generally dangerous and most reactionary terrorist the world has ever seen. Social Democracy helped, took over from the bourgeoisie the fraud of 'people's community' which had become historically impossible, and made of it a "theoretical system (economic democracy, "organised capitalism", etc.[9]). The German reaction could never have succeeded in doing what Stalin's henchmen achieved in the name of the Russian "socialist", and the Social Democrats in that of the "democratic" *people's community*.[10]

It was no accident that these same people invented the "popular front" after the catastrophe in Germany. They pressed the people into *parliamentary* community with their enemies, reducing the peoples demands to treacherous prattle, kept them away from every policy of their own, and cheated them out of the fruits of

---

9. History may be said to be repeating itself - the comparison with Tony Blair's "third way" for Britain in 1999 is self-evident. *Eds*

10. While in no way wanting to play down the role of the German Social Democrats and the 'Communists' as handmaidens to the rise of Hitler in their role of fragmenting, stifling and diverting the internal opposition, I feel that to this must be added the open support given to the Nazis by the governments of the rest of Europe who were vainly trying to manouevre Germany into a war against Russia (in accordance with the prescriptions outlined in Mein Kampf) by individuals from the European establishment, from Churchill himself to the Duke of Windsor, culminating in Neville Chamberlain's infamous "peace in our time" scrap of paper, all of whom, *post festum*, pleaded ignorance about what was going on in Germany, while at the same time investing heavily in the German armaments industry. However, what is known is that as early as 1930 Hitler was being funded by Henry Ford from America, and recent revelations with the release of official Nazi papers have revealed that the Ford Motor Company, one among 500 firms, ran factories in Nazi Germany with the use of slave labour from the camps, *esp*. Auschwitz (reported in The Guardian, 20/8/1999).

In Germany, specifically, the role played by the Catholic Church with its independent structure also cannot be discounted. *Eds*

their struggles. Only against these people can the indignant charge be levelled with sense and reason that they assumed the role of peoples tribunes, accepted the subjugated only "titularly" and limited the demands of the subjugated "to their consciousness". It requires a great deal of moral turpitude to make a historical leap to the historical Wagner and his historical spectacle while at the same time playing "Institute for Social Research" and advocating a highly critical, namely, a highly clever policy of "peoples community". The ideological expression of people's community is best furnished there by the representative of the new pseudo-science known as 'mass psychology'. This is Mr. Eric Fromm who uses one of the fundamental theses of the ideology of people's community as an epitaph to his book "Fear of Freedom", and thereby propounds naked government propaganda. The thesis about which the whole humbug revolves is Thomas Jefferson's statement: "Nothing is unchangeable but the inherent and inalienable rights of man!"

Unfortunately, these "inherent and inalienable rights of man", unchangeable as they may be when compared with the other commercial articles of the literary stock exchange, are peculiar. Apart from the speeches and books of apologist ideologists, they are nowhere to be found, and are therefore particularly suited to the "science" of people's community. And so the psychologising only serves to unmask itself when Adorno tries to pillory Wagner:

> "There is an early indication in him of a change of the function of the bourgeois category of the individual, when it tries to avoid annihilation in the hopeless conflict with social authority by taking sides with it and rationalising just this transition as its real individual development."

This 'very' accusation turns against the whole Institute for Social Research, whose background is the Washington government. In the hopeless conflict with the social authority, hopeless for the psychologists, that is, the Institute has taken sides with that authority. In this way, the 'critical' attitude turned into 'democratic' remedies, which, "rationalised as its real individual development", became nothing more than a masquerade for the mentioned treacherous transition. There is, however, a great difference between Wagner and Adorno. Wagner lived within a specific historical epoch and *exhausted the possibilities available to him.* Adorno, in contrast, lives at a time which in truth has arrived at the real consequences of Wagner's work and opens altogether different possibilities. Adorno now evades these new possibilities, (and that means only *necessities)* and, in so doing, is chiefly concerned with shirking the consequences of Wagner's work. It is full of spiteful vengeance against the one who sentenced the halfheartedness and narrow-mindedness of the 'centre' (of the Adornos) to historical doom *(Goetterdaemmerung)*, and whose prophetic vision grates on the nerves of this apologist for the ideological centre because it brands them as traitors from the beginning. This is why the crux of the Wagner question is timidly circumvented and buried under a great mass of crooked, distorted, or arbitrarily treated details[11]. The details themselves serve psychological criticism not for the clarification of the interconnections, but rather for the vindication of its own treachery, "rationalised" as criticism. Such criticism must defame Wagner's whole work in order to escape its conclusions. Only thus can Adorno's fury be explained when occasionally he blunders upon the crux of the Wagner question

---

11. Owing to lack of space, it is impossible to consider the bulk of these often grotesque details individually. One can, however, hope for opposition which would provide an opportunity to return to the matter - see footnote No. 7. [Needless to say, Adorno never rose to the challenge. *Eds*]

and must try to talk it out of the world at all costs. For example:

> "The conflict between rebellion and society is predetermined in favour of society. Finally, in the Ring, the supremacy of society over the opposition and the latter's functioning for bourgeois purposes are transfigured into transcendental fate. Such transfiguration alienates the world historical reality from real history."

As if the allegory had anything to do with 'real' history and were anything other than ....an allegory, in which symbolic splendour and 'transfiguration' are obvious as artistic, ideological, or other trimmings and can alter nothing. Incidentally, here Adorno already refuted himself in droll fashion when he calls Carl. F Glasenapp as a witness who has this to say about the allegory:

> He [Wagner] intended to exhibit in it only the hitherto existing historic phase of world development in its necessary doom, in contrast to Siegfried, the man of the future as he wanted him, fearlessly happy; and then he noticed how, already in essence in working out his plan, he had unconsciously followed an altogether different, much deeper, conception. It was not one single phase of world development, but the essence of the world itself, in all its conceivable phases, that he had perceived in his poetical composition and comprehended in its nothingness."

Adorno himself will later help us to clarify why Glasenapp interprets the symbolical significance of 'The Ring' in too limited a fashion, and why Wagner's radicalism drives him beyond the necessary doom. Meanwhile, the conflict between rebellion and society as pre-decided 'in favour of' society proves to be untenable, and the opposition 'functions' in Wagner's work by no means for 'bourgeois purposes', but only as the instrument of collapse (which can certainly be 'interpreted' as a bourgeois *end in itself*). Adorno is unable to get to grips with Wagner's conclusion and admit: it is the most profound conclusion to which a bourgeois can arrive. He does not tell himself that this conclusion has already become a grim reality and is absolutely unavoidable as long as the hitherto existing phase of world development has not been overcome. Instead of citing any historical or historical points of view whatsoever, he answers with aphorisms.

> It is the textbook case of what Lukàcs once called "flattening by depth": by levelling to what is in general human and thus - nothing; the 'essence' behind the appearance (viz. the law of motion of society), vanishes, and the distress of a historical epoch is hypostasised into a world principle."

Flattening by depth might be a witty aphorism if it were not identical with talking the world to pieces by psychology. Unfortunately, there as never been a historical "epoch" without distress. The most profound philosophy is therefore that which asserts that, at least in society and in organic life, distress is the ultimate law of motion. Adorno fails to prove *where*, by levelling to what is in general human, and thus nothing, the essence behind the appearance has been *missed*. Moreover, as Hegel has demonstrated, the essence must *appear* and in it everything special is in fact levelled and brought back to nothingness, as long the law of motion itself only confirms the nothingness of humanness. Our investigation will show in the proper place that Wagner was not in need of any psychological artifices in order to escape from the law of motion of society. On the contrary, firmly grasping this law, he demonstrates his profound insight by the genius with which he foresaw the nothingness of present society. Even had he been able to show a means of avoiding it, Adorno cannot cause the fact of the necessary collapse to disappear. Instead, he introduces psychology, which, as is clear from what follows, goes endlessly round in circles.

> "Yet this distress, as a concretely historical one, moulds the carriers of rebellion in the 'Ring' only too thoroughly. The opponents of the existing order are isolated individuals, destitute of all genuine compassion, and, moreover, of all solidarity: Siegfried, the man of the future, is a rowdy of obdurate naiveté, imperialistic through and through, at most with the doubtful advantage of grand-bourgeois lack of constraint over petit-bourgeois narrow-mindedness.

Adorno himself may decide whether a "rowdy of obdurate naivete", in spite of all doubtful advantages, does not also represent nothing but petit-bourgeois narrow-mindedness. But it seems an established fact that distress, even if hypostasised as a "world principle" cannot manifest itself other than "as a concretely historical one", whereby Adorno establishes himself as one who jemmies open doors. On the other hand, it remains uncertain whether Wotan's compassion for Siegmund, Siegmund's for Sieglinde hers for Siegmund and so on are "genuine" or not, because it needs a psychologist to decide that. What, however, is certain is the complete solidarity between Siegmund, Sieglinde, Wotan, and Brünhilde, which asserts itself just where Wotan is compelled to act against his own will and leave his "rebellious" protégé in the lurch.

Adorno arranges the matter according to his needs and accuses the "sovereign God" of his last misdeed, whereas the real conflict in Wagner stems from the law of motion of society which *strips* the god of all 'sovereignty' and subjects him to the will of Fricka as the representative of the existing order. Precisely where the solidarity between Brünnhilde and Siegmund asserts itself and both hold out to the end in rebellion against Wotan (in realty Fricka) with the subsequent saving of Sieglinde by Brünnhilde, Adorno inserts the dyed-in-the-wool 'imperialistic' Siegfried as proof of missing solidarity. And in this consists the trick of psychological criticism which, while defending itself, remains completely in the service of........'democratic' imperialism. This criticism is particularly keen on accusations such as imperialistic, treachery, 'terroristic' etc., but it has great difficulty in ridding itself of Wagner's all-round superiority. Adorno himself best shows how prophetically Wagner created, for example, Siegfried's 'imperialism':

> "Wagner's betrayal of the revolution is part of the revolution itself. Paradoxically enough, it is just the pessimism of 'The Ring' that contains traces of criticism of bourgeois revolution by unwillingly confessing that the rebellion of the child of Nature [Siegfried] leads once more into the entanglement with the given system; an insight which the present day admirers of Wagner and his type of 'elevation' would hear with dismay if the surging of the orchestra of the Goetterdaemmerung would let it appear at all."

To begin with, Adorno presents as "paradoxical" what, given the necessary collapse into nothingness, is once more self-evident. Adorno thus "unwillingly" confesses again that Wagner, despite entanglement in the given system, does not miss the law of motion of society, but makes it the axis of his whole drama; ergo: that he himself arrives, anything but "unwillingly" at the wisdom of his judgement of the hopeless nature of imperialism. Adorno cannot eliminate this wisdom and, in order to pass it off as 'unimportant' for Wagner's followers and for the whole world, causes the orchestra to prevent anyone's becoming aware of it, other than, of course, Adorno himself.

Let us, however, take, as a Wagnerian type of "elevation", the person of Mr Hitler, who cultivates Wagner and accepts the entanglement completely, up to and including the collapse. Thus considered, it has often happened that a pathologically criminal person played the organ after every murder, or went to bed in a funeral shroud, thus celebrating in the submission to the compulsion to commit crimes, submission to the last judgement

Like every other seer, Wagner could anticipate only the general trends of the movement, not the features of persons or the concrete circumstances. He has nothing to do with the details of the gruesome twilight of the Gods in the historical reality of our day But what possible sense has the reference to the surging orchestra of the Goetterdaemerung if Wagner's intentions are made absolutely clear by the course of the action and Siegfried's death? Is this reference not intended to mislead even those who hold the libretto in their hands? According to Adorno himself, the final version of 'The Ring':

> "[leads to the] desperate intelligence that he [Siegfried], in order to be more than merely a victim and servant of the existing world order, and yet unable to change its nature which moulded him and to which Wagner's resignation returns him, simultaneously, by his own annihilation and that of individuation, destroys that order itself"

The words "to be *more* than merely a victim and servant of the existing world order" once more throw a strange side-light on the previously mentioned "functioning of the opposition for bourgeois purposes."

In another place Adorno says:

> "In Wagner, the bourgeois class dreams of its own collapse as its sole salvation, yet without perceiving of salvation more than just the collapse".

That is not a bad description of what is now being experienced.: it is plain that Hitler, with his own annihilation and that of individuation, destroys also the existing world order[12]. However, it is not Wagner's "resignation" that calls the infatuated Hitler home into the existing world order which has seemingly lifted him above itself. Just the reverse: it is only the law of motion of bourgeois society, a society that of itself can find no way out of its entanglements. Thus Hitler appears as the illegitimate and "disinherited" true son of the Gods who rule the bourgeois world, just as Siegfried is the illegitimate (because begot of a common mortal woman) and disinherited grandson of Wotan. Both the disinherited (as mere executioners of the historical destiny thus also spiritually disinherited, of obdurate naiveté and petit-bourgeois narrow-mindedness) seemed appointed by fate to represent the 'new order', to negate the old law and to become

---

12. This should be read in conjunction with Weber's own statement above to the effect that the "seer [in this case Weber himself] could anticipate only the general trends of the movement, not the features of persons or the concrete circumstances." The "destruction of the world order" is all about us and only too apparent in the unnecessary deaths and suffering of millions of innocent people in genocidal wars (Ruanda, Bosnia, Iraq (where the continued bombing and deliberate starvation of food and medical supplies must be accurately and scientifically described as genocide) Croatia, East Timor, Kosovo, Chechneya, not to mention Vietnam). It s worth noting that since the end of World War II, the Americans have carried out saturation bombing on over 62 countries. There are also the phenomena of mass starvation (in the midst of plenty); the crippling of thousands of innocents by land mines; disease (mainly arising out of modern production methods esp. the over-use of antibiotics in animal rearing to the extent that 'superbugs - the ultimate unconquerable destroyer - resistant to every known antibiotic, are threatening that "medicine could be facing a return to the pre-penicillin days when all surgery carried the risk of infection and death" (Guardian, 6/9/99); feeding herbivores waste animal products (BSE); man-made natural catastrophes (floods, earthquakes etc.) brought about by global warming; the thinning of the ozone layer ......the list is endless.. *Eds*

'rulers of the world'. It is precisely here, in accordance with the law of motion of bourgeois society, that Wagner's verdict comes to pass: viz: Impossible! You are only material in the hands of the Gods who can only, by your death, end their own existence which has become insupportable.

Insofar as Wagner "resigns himself", he only expresses the law of bourgeois society, viz. that it can be freed from its own stupidity only by its own annihilation, and thus be led beyond itself. That is why it is a great mistake, as Adorno attempts to do, to make Siegfried in any way the allegorical representative of the 'proletariat'.

> "....Only in those exempt from the mythical tie of contracts and property, in the ignorant, can the idea of world history which passes judgement on this history, realise itself. 'Not soil and serfs I offer, nor father's house and hall: all I am heir to is my body, living I use it up.' The romantically sounding notion of the proletariat, which assigns to it the 'rescuing deed' because it is supposed to stand outside the societal guilt context, and which suppresses the dependence of the proletariat upon the mechanism of society....."

Nothing can be more false than to substitute the proletariat, for where, in the allegory, the disinherited petit-bourgeois appears as Wotan's own offspring, who, living, has nothing to consume but his own body (a matter of Hitler's pride). Further investigation will also make it clear that the allegation that Siegfried stands outside the social guilt context is no more than Wotan's crafty self-deception to which he confesses in his dialogue with Brünnhilde, and which Fricka prevents him from carrying out in the first round of their struggle. Nevertheless, the dependance on the mechanism of society retains its complete validity. Brünnhilde only carries out the deeper will of Wotan when she initially protects Siegmund and thereafter saves Sieglinde, i.e. Siegfried. Later, Wotan puts into Siegfried's hands the very weapon that previously, *in accordance with his plan,* would have meant nothing but a different ruin for Siegmund. But this does no more than complete the self-deception It is just the impossibility of escaping from the dependance that finally leads Wagner to his "desperate insight", that what "arises from what exists" must also disappear with it. Adorno is incapable of holding his argument together. Wagner had no need at all to transform the allegorical representative of the 'proletariat' into an 'individual' only *post festum* . From the start,, Siegfried is born as an individual in the sense of the petit-bourgeois fiction. If the proletariat is at all represented in the allegory, it is only in the nameless hordes of the Nibelung over which Wotan rules "not with contracts", but through the power of his spear.

Thus Adorno simply does not know what he is doing when he says:

> "Siegfried, once given the role of the immediate human being, no longer remains the allegorical representative of the class; he becomes an individual who alone, for Wagner, represents the immediate and natural human being. The revolutionary transforms himself into a rebel."

The truth, in contradistinction to this intrinsically flowery cant, is that Wagner needs the 'proletariat' only insofar as it has a part to play in *the historical* staging of the Goetterdaemmerung. As soon as this has come to its end, the 'proletariat' steps back into vague obscurity. For the rest, Wagner works through the circle of bourgeois possibilities, exhausts them, and allows the collapse of bourgeois society to be brought about *by itself.* Within the narrow limits drawn for him by the predetermined circle of bourgeois possibilities, Wagner disposes of the fiction of the petit-bourgeois individual who is never a 'revolutionary', but always only a rebel in that way.

Adorno's fabrications and varied 'interpretations' become more untenable with each additional step. At another point he says:

> "There is no way out of the infatuation context of society as long as private property is retained; under the sign of private property, subjective lust (love) and the objectively organised reproduction of social life are irreconcilable. 'Power', for Wagner the opposite of love, is, in the Rheingold, nothing other than the power of disposing of the labour of others, to be sure, with the nuance of blackening 'rapacious' capital alone."[13]

This only raises the question of where, in the Rheingold, the events of which occur long before the birth of Siegmund and Siegfried, the power to dispose of the labour of others can find a 'proletariat'. To whomever one assigns it (to the Giants or the Nibelung), Adorno cannot succeed in transferring the idea of the proletariat from there to Siegfried, the free child of Nature. Wagner was indeed the only 'romantic' who drove all that is bourgeois to its end, and thereby opened the way into the future. That is why, as long as the petit-bourgeois, whom the bourgeoisie considers only as its tool, could still only dream of its collapse, its ideologists acclaimed Wagner and changed Siegfried's rebelliousness, which to them was the revolution itself, into "salvation through collapse" without end. As soon as it became evident, however, that all rebellion within the bourgeois framework could only *throw into relief* the actual

---

13 "'With the blackening of 'rapacious' capital alone", only that of Wagner is intended. But Adorno would do better to direct this at, for example, Rudolf Hilferding, who prepared just this 'nuance' as a 'scientific' model for Hiter's use. As stated previously, there is a *direct* connection.

collapse, the high-flying intoxication changed into a hangover that perceived nothing but 'the collapse itself'.

While the masses must mutely resign themselves to their fate, the hatred of the 'rebels' is now directed against the one who, very early on, gave them a prognosis. It was only necessary to take this prognosis as seriously and consistently as Wagner himself in order to step out of the entanglement in rebellion into the real revolution by virtue of the fact that a law that has been defined loses its power. But missed opportunities only create redoubled hatred, more blind urge for self-vindication, more entangled 'rebelliousness'. The hatred of the ideologists for the one who rose from among them as executor of the testament of all rebellion and is flesh of their own flesh (Hitler) turns back upon Wagner. The rebels do not hold themselves responsible for Hitler, they execrate 'only collapse as the work of the one who was able to turn his own bourgeois contradictions into the colossal work of his allegory and present it to bourgeois society as a warning image.

This constitutes the mystery of the campaign against Wagner. Its pivot is the endeavour to destroy that revolutionary side which romantic art produced once in Wagner's neo-romanticism, and in it alone. In the words of Wagner himself:

> "In the progress of civilisation, so inimical to man, we can at least look forward to this happy consequence: the burdens and constraints it lays on what is natural grow to such gigantic proportions that in the end it builds up in crushed but indestructible nature the pressure necessary to fling them off with a single violent gesture. This whole accumulation of civilisation will then have served only to make nature realise its own colossal strength.......but the employment of this strength is revolution. It is the job of art specifically to reveal to this social

force its own noblest import and to show its true direction...."[14]

In the shadow of this campaign the mystery of the psychological writing of history too is revealed and its function as a secret self-defence against a guilt with which one burdens others. The case of 'Rienzi' with which this section was introduced already represents a brilliant psychological achievement. Before passing onto a broader examination Adorno asserted that Wagner, in Rienzi, no longer glorified 'free sensuality' but rather *denounced it*. Evidence:

> "A gang of young noblemen are on the point of making an assault upon the virtue of the chaste Irene."

This is the acmé of psychology, its highest level of perfection: the, so-to-speak, spiritual essence of the psychologist himself. To be able to present "an assault" on a young woman as a *denunciation* of "free sensuality" indicates at least a severe defect and a woefully distressing conception of "free sensuality", to put it mildly.. This being so, a strong warning against using such a conception is in order, whoever the victim, whether the chaste Irene or a wanton whore. Point of view of the defence: hatred of a superior leads to frenzy.

4.

Notes on the historical foundations for an appraisal of Wagner

It would lead us too far astray to investigate what Wagner's intentions were when he began the so-called glorification of

---

14. Bryan McGee. *Some Aspects of Wagner* (Panther)

bourgeois of all other countries.[15]

The question is now whether one will behave like a petit-bourgeois ideologist and reproach the wolf for having a wolf's nature, and condemn 'nationalism 'as such' bag and baggage. As long as the ideologist really turns against *all* wolves, he is still indeed a helpless petit-bourgeois, but remains morally clean.

What has to be understood, however, is that nationalism (including its weaknesses which are bourgeois from the beginning) was historically necessary and unavoidable, and has, indeed, where it appears without bourgeois weaknesses and degeneration, not yet played out its role. Except, therefore, where a nation really is still, or once again, suppressed, a thinking and honest person will oppose *bourgeois* nationalism which has exhausted its possibilities and openly carries the mark of degeneration on its forehead, and will, in every case, be resolved to fight nationalism wherever he comes across it. This must by no means be limited to the author of 'Deutschland uber Alles', for whom this poem had a meaning as different from Hitler's interpretation of it as the expression 'La Grande Nation' has when used by a French bourgeois revolutionary from that which it has when used by a French chauvinist.

Accordingly, historical truth, differentiations and nuances have always to be borne in mind. It should be noted in passing, that even were Wagner, who died when the swindle of the

---

15. The *name* for the typical debasement of the natural bourgeois national sentiment is not, as it happens, etymologically German, but based on the French model - Chauvin. There is not a single great capitalist country in the world which has not, up to now, produced the most repugnant chauvinists. Whoever does not at all times allow this truth to shine through, acts as a partisan of chauvinism.

Gründerjahre[16] was in full swing, to be burdened with all the sins of a bourgeois nationalist mentality, nevertheless, far more repugnant than he would be a Social Democrat who, among a thousand other misdeeds, supported the re-armament of Germany under Hitler and squeezed a series of pocket battleships out of the German people, the sinking of which by the erstwhile 'villainous Versaillese' he now frantically acclaims.

The depth of a guilt can be measured only from the level at which the perpetrator formerly stood. The higher the historical level and the greater the possibility of social progress, the deeper is the fall, the more wretched is the treacherous act. What an artist, a politician, a political party and so on were in reality is nowhere to be found in spoken words apart from work and action. It is often not even to be found in single works and actions, but in the total work, in the action *decisive* for the whole. Even the 'noblest' must fight for self-preservation, must err, and develop himself by means of his errors. When it comes to the *total achievement* of the *official* artistic, literary, religious, ideological, political, and other German leadership (the 'communist' leadership above all), it is found in its ultimate product - fascism[17]. Whoever in way attempts to lift the

---

16. The founding years of German industry initiated with the war indemnities exacted from France following the Franco-Prussian war of 1871.

17. In this and the following passages, the reader is reminded that the period of German history referred to comprises the events leading to the rise of fascism and the outbreak of world war II. The actions of the 'leadership', esp. the German Social Democratic leadership purporting to have the destruction of capitalism in its sights, so belaboured by Weber, may be exemplified by its voting of war credits to the German government in 1914 in direct contradiction to the resolutions of the Second International conference of 1912. *Eds.*

responsibility for this phenomenon off the shoulders of that generation of leaders which *confronted fascism during its lifetime* and tries to shift it on to history, the German people, the preceding generation leaders, or whatever, is a fraud.

Germany's political history in the narrower sense, the history of its ruling classes and governments may well be (to the special advantage of British imperialism) the richest on earth in mediocrities. Yet the world owes to the very narrowness, pettiness, wretchedness and *impossibility* of German conditions an array of great spiritual and artistic exploits such as no other country has to show. The great distress has forced into height what could not go into breadth. For the this the German people are to be neither praised nor blamed. It has undergone its great men, it has lived historically only through them and has itself remained featureless, formless, and without history.

Those juicy, round individuals, those persons of strong character, those penetrating political deeds - those truly 'epoch-making' ones with which, for instance, French history abounds, are extremely rare in Germany - timid attempts rather than unbreakable resolution, latent potency rather then immediate reality. The 'great man' appears in Germany, now as half or totally insane, now as child, hermit, or Don Quixote, now as rebel and weak character, now (as Marx said of Goethe) colossal and now philistine small. . Almost without exception, his *personality* is corroded by the dichotomy, ambiguity, corruption, and untenability of German conditions. They prevent him from solving the questions of the day and force him to turn to the solution of 'eternal' problems.

Not that ambiguities etc., would not be found elsewhere. Elsewhere, however, they are held in check; they are prevented by a series of single acts from gaining the preponderance characteristic in Germany. Emil Zola, for example, is a philistine who, examined 'psychologically', renders himself vulnerable to vicious analysis. A third rate artist and thinker, nonetheless, on the political stage, gives the impression of being a complete human being, whereas Goethe, a far more towering figure, steps with bowed back into the society of princes. Where England creates a world empire with tenacious brutality and knows how to keep it for a long time, the German bee-like industriousness leads from one national catastrophe to another.

The very conditions which constituted Germany's national misfortune, paradoxically supplied the German leadership with the best and sharpest weapons which people of progress ever held in their hands. An incalculable philosophical, artistic, political, organisational and pedagogic treasure; an army ready to fight and a host of sympathisers; an incomparably favourable situation, a sufficient material basis.....all that and much more lay in the hands of the German 'progressive' leadership of whatever colour, when the moment for action finally came for Germany. Germany's great men, they above all, by dint of unspeakable suffering, privation and persecution, in endless struggles with themselves and the hostile world and after experiencing terrible degradation and self-abasement, had come at last to the liberating conception and bequeathed it to those for whom the foretold better, more joyfully active future had become the order of the day.

The great moment found a wretched generation. A hammer in the hands of a sadistic killer, a robber, an idiot, a madman or a coward achieves different 'wonders' from those it does in the hands of a skilled industrious craftsman. The German intellectual, political, and literary leaders of the time before Hitler, if they are still alive, may choose their appropriate categories for themselves, but as soon as they try to escape from that and creep into the ranks of the industrious craftsman, the spirit of Richard Wagner will haunt them wherever they find their last refuge. Rising above his generation as a bourgeois among bourgeois and marked as a bourgeois in every respect, good as well as bad, he nonetheless achieved something which puts to shame every excuse given by the generations of leaders which followed him. This, as we have already noted, he achieved before the fledgling German imperialism had yet had an opportunity of 'testing its strength'. When the time came for it to do so, Wagner had already spoken his last word on the matter. In 1883, in Venice, Wagner left a world that had nothing more to offer him, nor he it.

For the betrayal of his achievements by the German leadership, for the exploitation of his work by the new German Wagnerians, he bears no more responsibility than does Marx for the atrocious falsifications perpetrated in his case by the same German (and international) leadership and by the ......fascists.[18] Marx could say of himself: "*Je ne suis pas Marxiste*", and Lenin: "I am no....Stalinist." And when Heine exclaimed: "I have sown dragons and heaped fleas", then he, Lenin, Wagner, Hegel and a hundred others of high rank would today, in view of the business ability of their 'followers', find it necessary to correct their 'error' in the following way: "We wanted men, and got corpse worms."

So much for the biography of Wagner whose personality is

---

18. It is useful to remember how Marx was not only slandered but also 'positively' exploited. With 'excerpts from the pamphlet 'On the Jewish Question', the Nazis made extensive propaganda against....the Jews. Nor were 'Capital' and other works spared. And who will dispute the fact that the falsifications of the Social Democrats provided the Nazis with excellent models, and that they, nevertheless, remained far behind Stalin?

otherwise of no interest in the present context.

5.

The Prophecy of the 'Ring of the Nibelung'.

There is, in Wagner's work, just as much and just as little fascism or 'late bourgeois terror' as there is in the hands of those who accuse him. With arguments for and against, with word plays, with interpretations of the plot, with childish, even silly, contradictions in the legends of the Gods, it is easy to argue and to 'prove'. It must, however, be constantly kept in mind that it is *society* that is terroristic, and that the absurdities (in a word) are inseparable from *all* fables and, further, from every play. These absurdities constitute an inexhaustible chapter on their own, as do their limitless multiplications in the context of private property and its apologists. Their inner connections and the fact that they are absurdities are brought to light by what may be, in the main, 'the decisive element'. Here, too, it often happens that some crucial feature masters the mass of nonsense; here, too, the general point of view expressed by a work says more about the real convictions, especially of the artist, than the artist is aware of. In the case of the 'Ring of the Nibelung', however, the matter is as simple as possible for anyone who has no need to hide his own guilt consciousness behind psychoanalysis, mass psychology, and similar deceptions.

That is why, in Wagner's estimation, every foolish nonsense is worth exactly the same as all the others and, above all, why he causes every single actor in the drama to be struck blind. Neither Siegfried nor Wotan is spared. Siegfried, the 'pure fool', only closes the 'circle of infatuation'. Wotan, on the other hand, had already lost half his integrity when he assumed his rule, and heaps one stupidity on top of another.

The stubbornness and exclusiveness with which Wagner treats the motif of general infatuation is astounding and of a force, truth, and prophetic power possessed by no other work of art which tries to grasp the nature of society and bring to light its fate. The 'prime cause' of bourgeois society, the secret of its existence, is revealed at the very start. Wotan, to carry out his plan, must use artifice and cunning. Without these 'resources', he appears completely helpless and powerless. The giant Fasolt shows him the limit of the so-called *'fictio juris'* upon which the rule of the Gods rest:

> "What you are, you are only as a result of treaties; your power is, properly considered, conditional

NB the treaties are a very doubtful matter. Wotan himself appraises them thus, for he does not spare himself the bitter truths concerning his existence. in his confession to Brünnhilde he says:

> When the lust of early love faded, my soul yearned for power. Driven by sudden wild desires, I made the world mine. Unwittingly deceitful, I became crafty, fettering what threatened ill.....The powerful whom we once held in check with laws, those whose courage we broke, these we bound to ourselves in blind obedience by fraudulent treaties.....

As Wotan won the world, so it melts under his hands. With each step designed to avert disaster, he is only led into deeper entanglement. Wotan knows this too, and proclaims the secret of his rule in his own way:

> But I cannot strike those with whom I have treaties; my courage would fail when faced with them. These are the fetters that bind me: the very treaties by which I became the ruler are now the ones which enslave me. I have handled

Alberich's ring - avidly I seized the gold. The curse from which I fled will now not leave me. I must give up all that I love, murder whatever is dear to me, crookedly betray whomever trust trusts me -- Away, then, with the imperial pomp, the divine splendour's glittering infamy. Let everything I built fall down in ruins. I give up my work except for the one thing that I still want: The ending - the ending!

6

Significance of the Infatuation Motif for our Time

If Wagner had left nothing behind but the baleful picture of bourgeois infatuation, our time, were it not affected by the same infatuation, would, to do him full justice, have to rank him among the greatest seers of mankind. He himself has been betrayed by those who accused him of betraying a revolution "that was not one at all." And yet, after the wretchedness of that revolution, he carried out one of the greatest revolutions in the history of mankind. The seventy years [one hundred and twenty-five. *Eds*] that have gone since the premiere of 'Goetterdaemmerung' have shown the infatuation context of bourgeois society in everything that lives and exists: in the upper world as in the 'underworld', in Wotan and Siegfried, in giants and dwarfs, in the decline of the Russian revolution, in the putrefaction of the Labour movement, etc.[18]

With the prodigious work which the bourgeois genius, Wagner, squeezed out of himself, (with all its flaws (which are, of course, those of the world itself)), he was in effect brought to the point society has reached with the catastrophic collapse represented

---

18 .A mere glance at the state of the world today (1999) completely vindicates Weber's judgement. *cf.* Footnote No. 12. *Eds*

by World War II [and subsequent events. *cf.* once again, footnote 12. *Eds*]. The inexorability with which he casts aside all interim solutions and wants only the "ending" which he has recognised as inevitable, is only now seen in all its impressive greatness. He produces no recipes, denies himself the tricks of 'organised capitalism', of the 'general cartel', of 'economic democracy' and other swindles[19]. On the contrary, he unmasks them uncompromisingly as bourgeois tricks which lead only more deeply into the network of infatuation and, as facts show, make the catastrophe still more inevitable. Wagner, therefore, is not one-hundredth part as stupid and treacherous as are his present day critics and those sages who, from an allegedly 'other than bourgeois' standpoint have given the world the swindles just mentioned. T.W.Adorno, for instance, perceives correctly:

> "In the midst of a distorted picture of community, the insight is won, however, which mercilessly strikes existing society in the face. Even the mythic entanglement of world history in the Ring is not only an expression of deterministic metaphysics, but posits at the same time the criticism of a badly determined world. Wagner's deciding the outcome in advance is identical with the infatuation-context of bourgeois society which proves itself most powerful where bourgeois consciousness fancies that it has raised itself to self-consciousness."

Although more might be said about the "distorted picture of community" (and where was Wagner to get an undistorted one for his drama?) and also about the deterministic metaphysics, the world has seen no better school than the one from which have come such perceptions and formulations. It is all the more tragic, then, to see how bourgeois infatuation shows itself in Adorno as well. All the achievements of Wagner, which he emphasises and

---

19. Once again, cf. especially Tony Blair's 'Third Way' for Britain. *Eds*

more or less adequately classifies, are subjected to the devaluing judgements of a psychology which makes the achievements suspect by casting suspicion upon their creator. It bristles with the sadistic drive to self-humiliation, with maudlin expiation, denunciation, self-denunciation, envy, the urge to destroy, twisted hatred (disgust at the fear of being recognised by some disgusting object at one with it), disordered feelings, and so forth. There is no motive, no phenomenon (be it love, humour, lust, or compassion), but is, upon being found in Wagner, at once interpreted and lastingly chalked up as subjective corruption, open or secret vice, or merely 'inferiority'.[20] In those dominated by the urge to squeeze the material into a preconceived scheme without distinguishing the various elements according to their specific weight, the several pieces of evidence selected from Wagner's life and work form no more than a picturesque jumble. The whole does not read like a treatise on a historical subject, sufficiently distant to permit a view of the general interconnections, the historical relations and their results, but reads like a breathless polemic written in the heat of a battle that lacks an actual opponent and serves only to appease one's guilty conscience.

As a result, the social research and the 'social character' of Wagner's work appears as the product of subjectively bad character traits, owing nothing to social conditions. It becomes self-evident then, that when *what is most important is not even perceived*, it cannot be properly classified.

> "In the gloomy context of the sentence pronounced by Wagner's work, one can see the revolutionary letters his work squeezed out of his character."

---

20. See again quotation from Hegel, op. cit. p.20. *Eds*

The main emphasis in Adorno always lies on the subjective "character" from which a work, God only knows *how*, squeezed something. But the task of social research should be able to show how the social character of an epoch permeates its interpreters; how the necessity shaping artistic, philosophical and other expressions of this epoch and its driving tendencies manifest themselves within the specific conditions in which individuals find themselves, how this necessity squeezes a *work* out of an individual, and does so only so far as the nature of the case allows, etc..

To the charge that Wagner pursues his victims (what possible sense can the word "victims" have?) down to their "biological fatality", Adorno immediately adds:

> "....because he recognised himself as one who only narrowly escaped being the image of a dwarf."

Thus Adorno pursues *his* victim into......biological fatality, a procedure essential for modern psychology.

Indeed: modern psychology, from whichever side one tackles it, reveals itself everywhere to be the foremost modern *ideological* attempt to anchor anew, in a pseudo-scientific way, the "guilt consciousness" (original sin) of Christian society which had been driven from all its hiding places. Society cannot exist without this guilt-consciousness because, with the fall of the guilt-laden victim, the god of private property would himself fall, just as the rich would with the disappearance of the poor. With totem and taboo, with Oedipus complex and biological facts of life, with individual and mass psychology, and with all such humbugs, it is by means of these that psychological systems transform individual guilt consciousness. dimmed by millennia of experience, into biological fatality. With the supposed psychological full consciousness, even those who had at least partially raised themselves to self-consciousness, are once more drawn into the circle of infatuation (cf. Adorno's remarks above).

It can be taken as read that this circle of infatuation must be paced out and exhausted not only theoretically, but also practically, before it releases the consciousness of man for the confrontation with 'scientifically' falsified basic facts. The 'peace' that will follow this war [World War II, *Eds*], will reveal a deception[21] and a delusion which undoubtedly will prove to have been most powerful at the place where, it was alleged, the philosophers stone had been found. The swindle of the pseudo-scientific theories in their latest form is certainly the last link in the chain of theoretical infatuation. The yawning spiritual emptiness of these theories, which try to paste together a world that is falling apart with spit, will be felt. They shout *immediate real* treason at a time when what is on the order of the day is no longer a 'new cognition' of the effectiveness of the 'treaties that are to be signed', the 'democratic' psychological system of Messrs Fromm and Company, but the deed, the carrying out of the Goetterdeammerung proclaimed by Wagner, the overthrow of the God who himself forms part of the compulsive mechanism of the system.

The undying merit of Richard Wagner is comprehensively to

---

21. We repeat: Weber's prescience here is quite remarkable. Since the ending of world war II, not one day has passed in which the salvoes of war have not been fired in anger. The United States alone have unleashed saturation bombing on over 62 countries, the quantity of bombs dropped on Vietnam alone in one day exceeding that dropped during the whole of WWII. War and production for war has become the mode of existence of bourgeois society, genocide its *ultima ratio*. See also footnote 12. *Eds*

have brought to light the nothingness, the premeditated deception, the even more foolish and clumsy entanglement of society in all the recipes contrived after the proclamation of the Goetterdaemmerung. The psychological and other objections to Wagner carry no weight at all. What has been proved right, however, is the merciless insight which causes Wagner to pass sentence, not only on an infatuated society together with it 'worker's movement' that has destroyed itself owing to this very infatuation, but also on himself - in this respect Adorno's words are correct, but in the wrong context. His achievement casts its dark shadow onto our age, absorbing and nullifying all that comes after him. It is the only achievement that goes beyond the bourgeoisie and its self-destruction. It marks the limit of the bourgeois capacity for cognition and thereby fixes the point at which consciousness, abused and corrupted by treaties, including those with Stalin, can rally itself again and find its direction in a society the downfall of which has become a tangible reality.

This taken into consideration, it is not only an anachronism but also an unjustified and incredible piece of nonsense to approach an important man like Richard Wagner, some sixty years after his death, from the standpoint of 'treason'. For, as often as one comes to talk about the only *allegedly* betrayed German bourgeois revolution, just so often does it show itself to have been no such thing. Not a single one of those taking part in it could alter the fact that the German bourgeoisie had to go through a development different from, for instance, the French. That is why no bourgeoisie on earth has produced from its midst a Wagner who applied to its system a prognosis so radical and so incisive in its historical reality. Even Marx and Engels, who had already set out upon the non-bourgeois road and were involved in the revolution, did not, after the end of the struggle, pass such wild judgements on those taking part in the unfortunate undertaking as T.W.Adorno, after seventy years of

Goetterdaemmerung, passes on the one who, in spite of everything, was the most revolutionary of them all.

Yet for our time nothing is so appropriate as the insight that *all* treaties concluded since Wagner are deception. But Wagner's importance is not limited to this. For the ones who have been deceived, it is not the scornful lack of concern with which Wagner tosses aside the zealous recipe makers and soothsayers and leads to the Goetterdaemmerung of our age - more important than that and a hundred other features of his work is his treatment and solution of the 'guilt question' which is of supreme importance for those who have been deceived. By this I mean that 'guilt' with which society burdens the individual and by means of which it keeps going to the day of its downfall. How can one explain the fact that T.W.Adorno does not even notice this *key* motif upon which Wagner's entire work is based and in terms of which it becomes self-explanatory? This is explained summarily by the circumstance already noted that modern psychology is nothing but a very fraudulent treaty with society which needs a continually renewed fixation of guilt as a *fundamental fact of the world* - this or that *actual* guilt is another matter .

7.

The First and Last Guilty One

That Adorno should be oblivious of how Wagner dealt with the question of guilt is the more astounding the more Wagner, from the start, unequivocally and decisively shows it to be the single determining impulse. Yet the way this comes about has its parallel in Christian theology. Systematic theology in its most highly developed form is willing, in certain circumstances, to jettison all religious dogmas and attributes of God. One thing only is stubbornly defended and that is the notion of original sin, whether in the shape of the 'ineradicably evil character of the world', as predestination, or whatever else it may be. The question of guilt as such is likewise taboo for Adorno who simply avoids discussion of it in Wagner's *work*. He ascribes guilt consciousness without qualification to Wagner himself and to biological causes. As a result what, according to him, might be termed the relevance of Wagner's achievement loses all connection with him and his evil character. It now resides in a mystical world called 'interpretation' to be brought to light by the subjective capabilities of the interpreter - we shall have an opportunity of observing predestination at work.

By comparison with this old complex, Wagner surely appears a strict determinist who seizes the bull by the horns and solves the problem in the natural way by driving it to its end. Liberation or "redemption" of the world from its evil is, for him, precisely what freedom was for Hegel: "cognition of historical necessity." Standing on a truly scientific level, he clings to the profound cognition voiced by Goethe, Kant, Hegel, Marx, etc. in their several ways: all that exists must, owing to its very nature, also wither away. However great the actual guilt may be, for instance, that of Alberic who steals the gold, it falls into the background and finds its explanation solely in terms of the *essence* of the world Wagner had to deal with. That is to say: this world collapses of its own motion.

There is no need of further information relating to T.W. Adorno since Wagner's insight can be *directly* used and grasped by anyone who is prepared merely to follow the narrative. In a quite simple and unique way, Wagner assigns the 'guilt' from which everything suffers *to the God and to those treaties the runes of which he has cut into the shaft of his world-dominating spear*. The Gods become a question of causality; what afflicts the world is its ruler and the institutions he protects, for, in contradistinction to the *'Creator'* of Christian legend and the 'inherent, inalienable rights of man' of mass psychology, Wagner knows only eternal nature and the God who has *usurped* the rule of the world.

However, where Christian theology entrenches itself behind the notion of original sin, or its equivalents, in order to save a God wholly without essence and properties, Wagner drives out even this empty remnant of him. In other words, he proves him to be a causal and transitory institution and consigns him to the historically actual fatality of his destruction; guilt will vanish from the world only when Valhalla has gone up in flames and consumed the Gods. Only then can the accursed gold be returned to the Rhine maidens and be reconverted into the innocent (neither good nor bad) tinsel that it was before a God entangled himself in its curse *through his own guilt.* Wagner's social allegory, simple as only genius could produce it, yet rich in subsidiary features, can nevertheless be correctly evaluated only if its subordinate features are taken into account in a completely objective fashion. The actual state of the allegory is as follows:

The Power and splendour of the gods rest (the word 'rest' underlines the causal connection) on their high-mindedness, their justice and their unequivocally honourable manner of acting. The social contrasts exist, depicted by the four spheres in which live the Gods, the giants, the men and the dwarfs, but so long as the Gods keep to their ideals, they remain the 'supreme' rulers. The four classes rarely come into contact with one another. Each class leads a life of its own, according to its tastes and needs. No class possesses something that another could covet; world peace is thereby assured.

Yet the Goetterdaemmerung has long been foretold. From the

outset Wotan has never been more than the *primus inter pares* among the Gods. Beyond the narrow circle of the Gods, he is powerless. To achieve his aims, he must, as already remarked, have recourse to artfulness and cunning. Why is this so?

Like every ruler-God, Wotan is naturally imagined as altogether aristocratic and noble. His high rank is dependent upon his great wisdom. This is the very hook on which Wagner hangs him and all the Gods of the world once and for all.

In order to achieve his great wisdom, Wotan has compromised himself and challenged destiny. Though long since chief of the Gods, he nevertheless, when young, 'sinned' by drinking from the forbidden spring from which comes all wisdom. If, on the one hand, he thus broke the original bond with Nature, so, on the other hand, he was punished for it with the forfeit of an eye in payment for the sacrilege. Moreover, proud and arrogant, he broke a branch from the world ash near the spring. From it he cut "the shaft of a spear" with which he henceforth ruled the world, and in which he cut the runes of the treaty which fettered the 'free' and compelled them to accept his rule.

All this is scientifically clear. At first, without protection against Nature, Man cannot help violating it in the course of his struggle for existence, "driven by wishes, sudden and wild". 'Someone', 'somewhere', must 'somehow' sully and violate the sanctity of the wisdom yielding spring and of the life giving Tree of Nature, if Man is not to disappear from the earth.[22]

---

22. Once again: only mass psychology can have the deplorable courage, in view of the tyranny of Nature over Man, to attain its desired end with the help of 'the inherent and inalienable rights of man'. Since it is especially concerned to establish the guilt of the German people, it is clear that, because of the 'alienation' of these 'inalienable' rights, the Germans must be

It is wholly in character that Wagner should remain at the level of this still valid philosophical and scientific perception of the 19th century. There is no *allegory*, and therefore no more easily obtainable perception which is more scientifically correct than Wagner's.

Whoever, driven by the struggle for existence, tries to gain knowledge breaks the original bond with Nature and confronts her[23]. In so doing, he *appears* in his environment to be the "fearless God" come "to drink from the spring." However, the price of the incipient knowledge which outwits Nature and tries to control its blind, demoniacal course and thereby conserve it, is the collapse of the pre-existing integrity of Nature, symbolically represented by Wotan's loss of an eye. The very knowledge that has assuredly made Wotan 'wiser' than everyone else is, however, the very thing that, owing to the loss of an eye, makes him incapable of perceiving other than one-sidedly, namely, prevents him from perceiving in time the consequences of his actions for the entirety of the matter they affect.

The question arises: what is the content of this 'incipient' knowledge? So far as this is concerned, Wagner in truth says nothing, since it is, to begin with, nothing but the subordination of nature to the needs of Man, made possible without 'human rights' after toil and experience from time immemorial. This subordination is, however, only *partial* (in this lies the meaning of the half-blindness) and for this very reason the inescapable perception of the possibility of controlling Nature of itself involves the equally inescapable compulsion to rule society (the

---

placed under tutelage and 're-educated'.

23. The reader is reminded of Wagner's own reflections on this question - see p.42 above.

world). Complete or all embracing knowledge 'at one stroke' is impossible. The knowledge that is only partial and splits the perceiver into a blind and a seeing half is therefore presented by Wagner not as a perception, but as an *act* which violates Nature. A part of Nature (the branch Wotan tears from the world-ash and shapes into an instrument of his rule) becomes separated from it and transformed into a means of its subjugation, Man himself being included as a part of Nature to be subjugated. From then on there is a gaping wound in the Tree of Life, and the source of cognition becomes troubled. Thus the Nornes sing:

> In the long course of time the wound destroyed the forest; the yellow leaves fell and the tree became dry and withered. Sadly, the water from the fountain dried; my song at this point became dark with sorrow. And if I no longer weave at the world-ash, the fir must serve for tying my line.

Thus, in the long course of time, primordial Nature is progressively devastated with the progress of subjugation, while a part of Nature and society either evade the regulating contract altogether, or can be made to conform to 'New Order' only by force. Mere partial domination of Nature must evoke the resistance of both the mastered and the un-mastered elements. Man and elements try all the more forcefully to avoid coercion the more the power and wealth of the ruling minority grow with increasing devastation. Wotan says of one of the elements, the fire God, Loki (a mixture of Hermes, Mercury, and Mephisto):

> Loki, who cunningly tempted me, has now wandered away and vanished.

About the same Loki, the Nornes say:

> Wotan tamed him with the spear's magic spell. He gave the

God counsel: he wore away his teeth gnawing at the runes of the shaft trying to discover how to set himself free.

That is now the outwitting of Man by outwitted Nature for the social counterpart of which the dialogue between Wotan and Alberic is especially characteristic:

Alberic:

> Beware! I know all your wiles; nor are your weaknesses hidden from me. You paid your debts with my treasure. My ring paid for the labour of the giants who have built your city. What you and the haughty ones long since agreed upon remains in force to this day by means of the runes in your ruling spear. You may not again seize from the giants what you have paid them as their price. You yourself would cause your spear to splinter. In your hand the ruling staff, strong as it is, would split like a straw.

Thereupon Wotan, with reference to the "double character" of his spear:

> The staff bound you by no runes of loyal treaty, you evil creature. Its strength brought you to your knees. I used it well when it came to war.

The essence of bourgeois democracy has hardly ever been unmasked more beautifully, more strikingly, more simply: Half of it consists of fraudulent treaties, which no sooner come into force than they become unworkable owing to 'circumstances' and have to be supplemented by cunning, violence, and lies; the other half consists simply of naked dictatorship. In stark contrast to T.W.Adorno's imputations, the attitude of all Wagner's characters, their way of speaking and acting the context of the action, etc., are permeated by a truly democratic concept which no bourgeoisie or social democracy on earth has yet brought to such a pitch of perfection. The most salient feature of this concept is that a true democrat ought, above all, to speak the whole truth about the status of democracy. All guilt belongs to the rulers. If the first, and elementary guilt, as the compulsion to subjugate nature and as the compulsion to rule, is unquestionably *self-evident*, and therefore, *as guilt*, need not be discussed, nevertheless the *eternal contradiction* between nature and society is set in motion by the ruler, as the *historical antagonism* between society and nature, individual and society. It is the ruler who transfers this antagonism into the dialectic of progress and retrogression, equality and inequality, cognition and infatuation, and all other pairs of opposites.

Private property over nature and the power to dispose over man who belongs to nature are irreconcilable with the essence of the whole. The *actual* or debatable guilt thus begins where what has developed has gone beyond the conditions heretofore existing. From then on valid treaties and violence can no longer stop the development: violence alone becomes the only resource. The first result of this is, of necessity, the splitting of the ruling clan into a cautious (conservative) part, and another striving for the expansion of power.

Is it accidental coincidence or intention?.....Whatever it is, it is the instinct of genius that makes Wagner, with an assured touch, start the action and conflict at this very point.

The time has come for the theft of the Rheingold; the long since foretold end of the gods announces itself as the consequence of laws which have become historically effective. Genius, nothing but genius, makes Wagner conceive of 'Rheingold' as having no breaks between the acts, the changes of scene which usher in the various spheres of society being marked only by musical interludes. This is the scientific and rational indication that the following events belong together and condition one another. The theft of the Rheingold and the completion of Valhalla happen simultaneously. When Alberic disappears with the gold into the depths, the completed Valhalla appears in the splendour of a new day. This signifies that the basis of Wotan's rule is shaken at the very moment at which the power and splendour of the Gods reach their peak, crowned by Valhalla, their symbol.

But Wotan might yet overcome Alberic who seeks to gain 'the world's inheritance' by means of the ring, *were he still free within the framework of his own order.* Whether Wagner was aware of it or not, it is Hegel's penetrating insight that shapes the matter: Wotan's power does not collapse owing to some external force; it does so owing to its own nature. Beginning and end, perfection and decay, interpenetrate - perfection contains within itself the poison of a deadly sting A determinable boundary between perfection and decay does not exist. With the last 'free' contract, that is to say, the contract roughly in line with existing conditions which Wotan concluded with the Giants, his deep-rooted dependence and the ruin of his rule became already starkly visible. This is in the nature of all things; by their immanent limit, they are driven beyond their limit and are destroyed. As Wotan, the one-eyed sage, rejoices at the sight of Valhalla and sees his will become reality, he appears as a sage who is at the same time.....not a sage. This is the hook, as previously remarked, on which, with Wagner's consent, he hangs himself.

For the point about which the whole conflict revolves, and which T.W.Adorno has totally neglected, as he has so many other things, is the fact that the Gods can achieve the perfection of their splendour only on condition of *giving up their youth.* The *quid pro quo* which the giants exacted *by treaty* for the building of Valhalla is part of the very nature of Godhead itself - the Goddess of youth. A profound thought: the peak of maturity is one with the definitive onset of decay. The time for the implementation of this article of the treaty comes with the accomplishment of Wotan's will. Nothing he can now do to preserve the youth of the Gods can delay the carrying out of the sentence. Ruses, cunning, praetorian guard, breach of treaty, faithlessness, fraud, and even Siegfried can at best determine only the *actual process* of aging. The utmost that the deluded Wotan himself can possibly achieve and, in Wagner's work, actually does achieve is the acknowledgement of the historical destiny. Just as, after the break with unconscious nature, all perception makes a detour via the social processes, so Wotan as well, in like manner, regains his sight. He is 'free' only insofar as he bows to the historical necessity and finally *wills* it.

> So have my blessing, son of the Nibelung. What thoroughly disgusts me I give you as your inheritance - the empty splendour of the Gods.

How consummation and destruction interpenetrate; how the given organism transgresses it limits; how this transgression manifest itself in the splitting of the ruler's will, one part striving after "mature maintenance" (conservatism), the other trying to counter decay by the expansion of power (reaction); how this accentuates the basic conflict instead of mitigating it, etc., is brilliantly depicted in the dialogue between Wotan and Fricka:

Fricka

> The castle pleases you but makes me afraid for Freya. It is finished and the bond must be redeemed. Have you forgotten what you pledged?

Wotan

> I fully remember all that those who built the castle demanded. I brought the defiant ones to heel by means of a treaty, so they built me this splendid castle. There it stands, thanks to their strength. As for the price, do not heed it.

Fricka

> If I had but known of this bond, I would have prevented the fraud. But you gladly turned away from us in order to deal with the giants yourself, free from our interference. By this means you shamelessly gave away my beloved sister, Freya, and were even happy with the wretched business. What, then, do you men still hold holy and dear to you when you seek only for power?

Wotan:

> And did not Freya show the same eagerness when she pleaded for it to be built?

Fricka:

> Worried about my husband's fidelity, sadly I was forced to consider how to hold him to me when he felt moved to go away. A beautiful home, and charming fittings I thought might serve as gentle bonds to keep you here at rest. But, to you, this home meant only schemes about ramparts and resistance. These would but increase your power and might. The towering castle was built only to bring about a more raging storm.

Wotan:
  (smiling)

> If you want to keep me in this stronghold, you must make it possible for me, immured as I am, to conquer the world. Movement and change are the breath of life and I cannot do without the play.

During this charming domestic scene all the family skeletons do indeed emerge from their cupboards. Broken and forgotten treaties characterise the reign of the impotent Wotan. Though he knows that the Goetterdaemmerung is brought nearer owing to this, he still has no intention of keeping his promise. From now on he is disgusted to find that, whatever he does, everything always comes back to him. Appearances notwithstanding, Fricka, this amalgam of Juno and Offenbach's 'public opinion', at bottom wants the same as Wotan, but she sees the weak point and tries to avert the danger in her own way. That is why this guardian of "marriage and oath" is the one to cry the loudest for .....the breaking of treaties, for which, of course, the 'moral' justification is not lacking. The only self-evident thing is, once more, the natural one: public opinion exists exclusively for patching up the cracks appearing in society, and it lies in the very nature of the matter that it should as a result overwhelm its creator. Wotan is, in every conceivable respect "enslaved by his treaties", caught in his own noose.

And so it comes about that the whole action takes place under the sign of the God's guilt; Siegmund and Siegfried will neither save themselves nor "man" from guilt. On the contrary, they will, in the first place, save *the Gods* and finally, once Wotan admits to having deceived himself, purge the world of the guilt of the Gods and bring about their destruction. God is the first and last guilty one. The grandeur and unique importance of Wagner's achievement lies in his having given the central place to liberation from the representative of private property in the world who allows himself to be driven out for good *by means of this very institution.* The individual features of this achievement can be classified and correctly, i.e. properly, evaluated only if judged from this standpoint.

8

Wagner's Historical Position, his Mission and its Latest Results

The history of God is the annihilating criticism of God: *his* world is also its judgement. Such a cognition, if as consistent and radical as it is in Wagner, suffices to bring to light those forces which, according to T.W. Adorno:

> "....are released in Wagner's work in the early period of bourgeois decay".

This refers to those forces which, in agreement with the formulations of the world's best school so far, Adorno calls *the possibility of another society* which the existing and *decaying society develops within itself.* The passage referred to in Adorno reads as follows:

> "But if the decaying society develops in itself the possibilities of the other which may at some point take its place, it follows that Nietzsche misjudged the forces which are released in Wagner's work in the early period of bourgeois decay: in this lies his injustice to Wagner. There is no element of decay in Wagner's work from which there has not sprung a burgeoning of something new."

The important point here is that more than this could not be asked of Wagner in his day and still less could it be today. He did what he could and only a rogue would wish to do more. If what he did does not constitute the future itself, then it is its indispensable precondition in that it acts as a forcing ground for the burgeoning of the new that springs from the destruction of the present. That is why the historical sequence of which Wagner forms a part always remains the same. Before Wagner there are the great Utopians who appear in those countries where bourgeois society is developing. They see the evil of this society already in its very beginnings, but they want to cure it by means which are *not yet developed out of itself.*

The next great landmark in the course of bourgeois development is the unique phenomenon of Wagner. He appears in the country of half-measures and late-comings and perceives, beyond vacillations and single actions, that nothing, literally nothing, can free the world from its ensnarement other then the removal of God and the system upon which he is based. That is the real content of the supposedly 'inflated' notion of the redemption of the world in Wagner. Whether he lets redemption take place in ecstasy or asceticism after the pattern of 'Death and Transfiguration' or in a mixture of twenty different kinds of neuroses, remains irrelevant with regard to the state of affairs itself. Social research would have the task of explaining ecstasy and asceticism, but not of condemning them psychologically. For if what brands society is insecurity, the neuroses are once more self-evident, and so long as there is no element of decay that does not show the promise of the burgeoning of something new, the 'redemption of the world' remains thoroughly realistic.

Wagner takes his destruction and that of society seriously. That is what makes him fruitful, makes his achievement genuine, and gives him and every other bourgeois the right to celebrate the giving-up of himself in the allegory as a heroic act which the honoured bourgeois ideologists need only to emulate in order to clear up all their contradictory urges. At the same time, however, the consistent giving up of what is bourgeois is what makes Wagner unique, and counterposes him to two large groups which appear before, with, and after him.

The first group is that of the honest but narrow idealists, quacks, charlatans, etc., who have achieved fame under the names of Proudhon, 'German Socialists', Fabians, Dühring, etc. The second group consists of those who, after the success or failure of the bourgeois revolution, could be the only *objectively possible* traitors. There are the pretentious, partly educated, partly illiterate, partly brutal and violent persons who can be found in the lists of the leaders of the Social Democratic[24] and 'Communist' parties of the world. These are the ones who have strangled real revolutions,[25] have perpetrated real acts of terror, and psychological violence, and have brought about the chaos. Both groups overlap, and have the social function of upholding the context of blindness and delusion, of renewing it and exhausting it both theoretically and practically in detail.

---

24. Up to and including Tony Blair, Prime Minister of Great Britain, to this day with his absurd soubriquets of 'New(!) Labour', 'The Third Way', The 'Moral High Ground' etc. etc. *ad nauseam*. Especially significant is his statement at the 1999 Labour Party Conference: "It is time to move beyond the social indifference of right and left, *libertarian nonsense* (our emphasis. *Eds*.) masquerading as freedom". (Guardian 29/9/1999). Could there be a more thinly veiled threat that dissent, whether from 'right' or 'left' is not going to be tolerated - mere '*libertarian nonsense*' and in addition we have the formation of a special information dissemination unit directly from the Labour party quite clearly modeled of the Third Reich's Misnistry of Propaganda. Behind this stands the figure of Alistair Darling, Tony Blair's press secretary, ghost speech writer, and spin doctor, possibly the most dangerous man in the political spectrum - why does the name of Joseph Goebbels spring to mind?

25. cf. especially: the behaviour of the Communist Party in France during the uprising in Paris in May 1968. *Eds*

If therefore, as T.W.Adorno admits, Wagner fairly plausibly "compared himself to the interpreter of dreams rather than to the dreamer", then it must be admitted that he interpreted the dream better and more profoundly even than Marx, who supposed it possible that the new society could be achieved before the blindness and delusion to which bourgeois society gives rise had exhausted themselves with the self-destruction of that society.

The failure of all revolutionary endeavours owing to the blindness of the leadership, insofar as there was not simply treachery, is, up to the present day, a fact which, in the interest of the future, has to be acknowledged without qualification. Thus the first demand to be made upon 'interpretative', i.e. creative criticism, is:

Take the given facts into account, whomsoever they concern. Keep in mind the abiding insight that "one can't do without the play". Clear the ground, for the significance of word and action changes together with time and conditions: great works, above all, reveal their range only in the light of the present that alone can show how much the teeth of time have been able to gnaw away. Look for the essence of the work; make no claims that lie outside the matter. For, in the end, the accusation that a critical attitude springs from resentment is justified only where the criticism, as in the case of Adorno, is the product of delusion and clouds the issue.

Upon these grounds, we judge in favour of Wagner: his genius not only combines the dominating themes in the Rheingold and for the most part reduces everything to 'Leitmotifs', but also causes these to become transformed into historical forces which, in the course of ages and without regard to Wotan's plan, acquire the definitive form that brings about the twilight of the Gods. Adorno, too, confirms this in typically distorted fashion when he notes about Wagner:

"The imperialist perceives the catastrophic character of imperialism in a dream; the bourgeois nihilist has an insight into the very heart of the bourgeois urge to self-destruction that is to come in the epoch following his. At the end of his late essay 'Religion and Art' he says: 'Progress in the art of war more and more turns it away from moral source to the improvement of mechanical means: here the wholly unadorned power of the most primitive natural forces are artificially brought into play together, a circumstance which, notwithstanding all mathematics and arithmetic, may permit the blind will to intervene one day in its own way with elemental force. Already the armoured monitors, which the proud and splendid frigates can no longer withstand, offer us a spectral, gruesome sight: dumb, resigned human beings, who no longer look like human beings, serve these monsters and are no longer willing to desert from the horrid boiler rooms: yet, as everything in Nature has its destructive enemy, so art creates as well torpedoes in the sea, everywhere dynamite cartridges, and so on.[26] One can no longer doubt but that all this together with art, science, gallantry, honour, life and possessions could be blown sky-high one day owing to an unpredictable mistake.'"

A gift to Adorno from the bourgeois (finally the right word) "nihilist" and the "imperialist", since Wagner, as one who "sees through" has already disposed of both of these categories: but was not this "seeing through" the bourgeois urge for self-

---

26. And what an 'and so on', the horrors of which Wagner could never even have begun to dream, could the list include today, from cluster bombs of land mines to 'tactical' nuclear weapons, bacterial and chemical agents, hydrogen bombs capable of destroying the planet, and now the products of nano-technology capable of silently and without warning wiping out whole populations within minutes. *Eds*

destruction in the epoch after his Wagner's true mission? Indeed, he who could say of himself: "I have completed my mission victoriously," remains today the sole victor after the interval of time during which his tetralogy is transformed into actual bourgeois reality. The completion of the social drama nears its end..

'Already' the races or tribes of the world are swinging back over Channel and ocean to the Rhine to win the ring of accursed gold for themselves. Adolf Hitler comes forward as the 'Siegfried' of historical reality who, as the duly installed hero of Wotan (the big bourgeoisie), always "triumphed before he had fought"[27]. Hitler, then, this narrow petit-bourgeois who has gone wild and is the caricature of the nature-child, will be killed in the modern hunting with aeroplanes and tanks as assuredly as was Wagner's ideal character. The ensuing scuffle among the merry hunters and their mutual killing over the possession of the world dominating ring will not be long in coming. In the general chaos, the unchained elements will possibly, like the Rhine, rise above their banks, join in the roaring conflagration and also drag down to the depths the sinister super-Hagen of the Kremlin. In any event, and in whatever way the conflagration might be brought to Valhalla, the blind will has definitively intervened and will not rest until it has buried the Gods under the ruins of their splendour. In the midst of this ever-widening devastation, the task is to establish on firm ground the perception which bursts through the closing circle of blindness and delusion and which remains after all that tormented humanity has endured through honest effort and disgraceful treachery.

---

27. Adorno uses this as an 'objection' against Wagner, whereas it is in full agreement with his conception of 'pure execution'.

It must be stressed: how infinitely superior, more farsighted, more courageous, more honest and more profound was Wagner with his merciless expulsion of the guilty God in comparison with the multi-coloured apologists for the Christian world order as the only dispenser of blessings, and against which Wagner aimed his crushing stroke. The God of private property, not the work of Richard Wagner, is simultaneously the creator and only too willing "prophet and bailiff of imperialism and late bourgeois terrorism." He and nobody else was, in early times, the first terrorist; nobody else will be the last. It was he who teutonised the whole world in the most barbaric manner, who has subjected Japan, China, Africa, India, the happy children of the South Seas, in short, all the ravished and hounded-to-death coloured peoples together with all flora and fauna to the searing curse of the Ring of the Nibelung.

But something else must be especially insisted upon today, when the historical circle around England is also closing. It is, in fact, not the 'Germans' east of the Rhine who have unleashed the *furor teutonicus* bred by Christianity., but the original teutonic Anglo-Saxons on the Thames. They have been its most reckless and merciless pioneers who smothered all resistance with blood and fire. It is once more they who have taken the most furious and cruel part in the Christianisation of North America, always ready to wage war against and to enslave their own brother pioneers. And it is they who now (poor Europe) swing back across Channel and Ocean to the Rhine and burden the bled-white peoples with a responsibility which can be nothing but a camouflage for their own bloody crimes.

Should England and America, when, for the second time after victory they have the fate of the world in their hand, laugh in complete blindness and delusion at the threateningly raised hand of the felled 'Siegfried', should they toss aside Wagner's challenge to them to emulate the guilty Wotan with a great gesture of resignation, then all the more terrible will be their ruin and all the more will it remain true that Wagner destroyed the myth on which society feeds - the myth of the innocence of God and the guilt of his creatures. If nothing is saved from chaos other than the perception that private property and its institutions are the sole culprits who hold humanity in their iron grip, and delude and ruin it through the coercion exercised by their system, then the most important link with the future will have been preserved,

9.

Psychological Coda
(Satire after the Tragedy)

In order to make this perception victorious, a bitter struggle must be waged against all conscious and unconscious attempts to befog it anew. One already knows: bourgeois society cannot do without anchoring guilt consciousness in God's *creatures,* whose redemption on penalty of eternal condemnation is not made dependent upon God's *disappearance*, as with Wagner, but upon His 'grace'. Miserably wasting away, the bourgeoisie tries to implant guilt consciousness in a thousand ways, some clumsy, some skilful, and it has found, to its own consolation and to the renewed injury of its victims, a new method, a new opiate, in the form of *modern psychology*.

The weak spot of this psychology is most easily revealed in its applicability to any given.....psychologist. For there has never been a psychological analyst who was not himself in need of analysis, and that is why modern psychology has to be defined as a form of petit-bourgeois ideology. It is characteristic of such ideologies to be a hodge-podge of all possible and impossible fields of knowledge and, even more, a compendium of ignorant platitudes. This was already noted, in his own way, by A. Lange, who considered the critique of psychology to be an undertaking by which "the largest part of the 'science' would be shown to consist of babble and deception." The self-deception, in the days of Lange still a highly cultured affair compared with the prestidigitations of today, is what matters. Its methods and results being applicable to everything, it yields everywhere the same, and therefore - nothing. In this self-deception, the petit-bourgeois, simultaneously dependent and vengeful (Arthur Koestler is a fine example) communicates to all others his disappointment with the world and therefore he can feel comforted. For the operation consists in bringing all people of character finally so far down that the psychologising petit-bourgeois finds himself 'on the same level' as every genius, can piss with him into the same dirty gutter, and from this derive justification for the familiarity of calling him 'pal'.[28]

The omnipresence of complexes and symbols inherited from biology, anthropology, etc., on the one hand excuses everything and, on the other hand opens the possibility for self-righteous wretchedness to indulge in the feeling of 'superiority' and to cast suspicion on the fortes of its neighbour with the help of the inferiority of wretchedness.

For this reason, and quite in accord with the scheme of the *unfulfillable* commands of Moses, modern psychology is nothing but the 'scientific' substitute for the auricular confession which 'reveals' to the analyst the 'most secret' thoughts of the suffering patient which are tacitly assumed as known. It is only necessary

---

28. Hegel referred to such psychologists as the lackeys of history, and observed that "no hero is a hero to his valet, not, however, because the hero is not a hero, but because the valet is - the valet...." *Hegel, Phenomenology of Mind*, trans. J.B.Bailee.

to place these unfulfillable commandments side by side to have at once, leaving aside sanctioned crimes such as war, pillaging, or the extermination of whole peoples etc., the hackneyed result to hand: I commit adultery, you are guilty of calumny, he embezzles, it onanises, we fornicate (look in vain for a brothel), etc.

In addition it must be said regarding the psychological legislators: You go astray and totally misunderstand. Like the priest who, after giving absolution, goes to confession himself, and there again tells only what is well known, so at every street corner there awaits you the avenging analyst who knows your most 'hidden' thoughts before you have revealed them.

Here it is worth remarking that there is a perception beyond the doom pronounced in the 'Ring' which Wagner brings out in 'Parsifal'. It is not an 'original' Wagnerian thought; indeed Freud was once close to it: *The wound can be healed only by the shaft of the same spear the point of which inflicted it.*

In the modern version, based upon the present state of science, this old idea of 'redemption' of the world by a definable and actual means would read the evil is *temporary*; it lies wholly within the historical process and it carries in itself the formal means for its overcoming.

Of decisive importance for judging modern psychology as a form of mere ideological fraud is the fact that it is precisely because psychology has extended its field to include sociology that this fruitful insight is 'repressed' so far as society is in question and instead finds its place in the realm of 'abstractions'. From now on the wound is no longer caused by the actual social struggle for the emancipation of man from Nature; it is ingrained rather as an irremediable 'original sin' in biological and anthropological facts, which, for their part, are made to *determine* the social process. This procedure is in no way altered if one gives the swindle a 'positive' turn and presents the unchangeable, inherent, and inalienable 'rights of man' in the metaphysical abstract threadbareness of the Institute for Social Research. 'Redemption' is finally, parallel to the 'reason' of bourgeois revolution and to the 'divine act of grace' of Christianity, only a matter of psychological analysis which, over the heads of the many who are called, is always practised only by the chosen few. However, chosen for aeons is only the one who has boldness, arrogance, and stupidity enough to claim that he is in possession of a 'reason' or divine grace which is supposedly *independent* of actual conditions.

From the multitude of problems and objections which must spring up here quite naturally there is but one way out that puts everything in order - the recollection of the dictum that practice is the criterion of truth. What psychology achieves in social research can easily be seen in its dead fruits. Thus argument once more falls back into parody and, together with Loki, lands us once more on Shakespeare:

"Sweet are the uses of adversity."

That is the Ariadne thread that leads the way through practice and compels the 'art of interpretation' to end as it began: with struggle for the natural and self-evident. Art and freedom of interpretation, as they have been exercised here, lead first of all to the statement that they too.....were not what they pretended. They renounced the unfounded freedom which the psychologist assumes to be his. They limited themselves to the elaboration of the fundamental traits and made clear who, from the sequence of oppositions, emerged as the victor in practice. On the *bourgeois* side the only victor was Richard Wagner and the conclusion can only be: if not already born great, Wagner *achieved* true greatness - he who was no rogue and did only what he *could*.

Having arrived at this point, the dead Wagner seizes the living Adorno. What do Adorno's numberless approaches and objective blindness to Wagner amount to? Factually, to neither more nor less than the suspiciously emphatic reproach that Wagner did *not* act like a rogue, which means: he ought to have done *more* than he could and *incomparably achieved*.[29]

One might expect that the critique that raves in this way would, sixty years after Wagner's death, at least be in a position now to offer *of its own* that 'plus' it demands of him and which, in the meantime, has become - more than possible. But far from it. Firstly, the critique falls far behind Wagner and consequently even farther behind that plus which has now been long in existence; secondly, its remedy revolves about vague recipes and consolations for which it has branded Wagner, following the thief's method of crying: "Stop, thief!" Certain orators may be 'admired' because on every occasion they talk themselves into the mire. In order to convince oneself of the hopeless ad-miredness of psycho-analytical attempts to deal with social phenomena, one may take the passage already quoted (p.69) which refers to the forces which, in the early period of bourgeois decay, already manifest themselves in Wagner's works.. This passage speaks volumes. With "but if" and "then", it shows a rogue of a special kind, that is, one who voluntarily keeps himself balancing on the razor edge between perception, and blindness and delusion.

---

29. This incidentally, is the attitude of all those ignoramuses who, deeply dissatisfied with themselves and the world, present themselves as 'fine fellows', have much critical feeling, yet never come up with a single idea of practicable applicability.

Justice must and shall grant him: the revolution which the Social-Democrats and 'Communists' really did betray has, as a result of this, landed him in a very uncomfortable position. Originally not evilly disposed, he finds himself in the midst of the hopeless disintegration of the workers movement, of democracy, etc., without social support for his convictions and without real perspective. He censures Wagner who had excused his lack of contact with the political ferment of his day on the grounds of the "ideal core of his attitude" Yet his reproach has a great blemish; he is in the same position himself and with the purely 'investigative', theoretical, academic, declamatory attitude of the 'Institute for Social Research' which has been going on for years, he flies from the political ferment of the day much more than did the accused. He knows where the solution lies, but he does not know what, if he were to do anything at all, could drag him down or push him up. He would like to go in the right direction but something could then happen to him, so he sacrifices his character and tries to be in two places at the same time. He arrives at "a sort of rehabilitation of the Wagnerian nihilism" and discovers in it many features which are progressive and show the way forward. But as he misses the *essential* feature, so also his ceaseless denunciation of Wagner, denunciation being the very thing for which he eagerly reproaches Wagner, never passes beyond innuendos and very vague formulations of the features in question. As *his* decisive finding he gives, at the end, an oracular revelation which, imperialistic through and through, lies in the sphere of psychologically prepared democratic-mystic consolation. It is redemption by a leap into the imagination that leaves everything as it is under the protection of the Allies and acquiesces in the grace that as led it to capitulation before the ruling powers.

After Adorno has quoted the conclusion of Wagner's late essay on 'Religion and Art', which deals with the possibility that "owing to an incalculable mistake all this could be blown sky-high one day", the reader finds, coming doubly unexpectedly after such words, the following assertion:

> "But[!] of this [i.e. of being "blown sky-high"! J.W.] Wagner's music knows more than the word."

This assertion becomes ten times more astounding if one recalls the circumstances on which in truth Wagner's *word and allegory* are based. These circumstances speak of nothing else except of the necessary downfall, of the annihilation and of the "being blown sky-high", indifferent to anything else, including psychology. If this is, one the one hand, the point which gives Adorno the opportunity for manifold objections of a psychological and philosophical nature, he cannot, on the other hand, completely ignore it as the core of Wagner's conception., to which he adds, to be sure not only "paradoxically enough" but also with stupefying naiveté, a suddenly deeply dissatisfied "BUT".

Now savour a last example of the contradictory urges of psychology. Adorno begins the concluding section of his investigation with the words:

> "Wagner brings to light the early stage of bourgeois decay."

That sounds 'objective' and is supplemented by the words:

> In the allegory his urge for destruction anticipates that of society."

This, in its turn, makes the assertion about Wagner's music "knowing more" completely incomprehensible, since, in the *allegory*, the matter is made absolutely clear. In it, the *words* testify to the knowledge of being "blown sky-high" as unmistakeably as does the conclusion of the quoted essay.

What, then, is rotten in the Institute? This:

Adorno holds, vis-a-vis Wagner, a psychological, i.e. totalitarian standpoint. It is the claim to exclusiveness on the part of modern psychology which, as a real ideology with an uneasy sense of its own weakness, demands: All *or* Nothing. But this "or" regularly turns in its hands "and" - All *and* Nothing. The beautiful objectivity of the early period of bourgeois decay is surreptitiously disposed of; now it is Wagner's or "his work's" urge for destruction which in the allegory anticipated that of society. Despite all his half-way (*en quelque sorte*) 'rehabilitation' of Wagner's nihilism, simultaneously denounced as 'Utopia', and despite a flash now and then of insight into the real nature of the matter, the author acts too much in self-defence to be able to cope with Wagner. The result is clear: Wagner's quite *consciously* and carefully designed basic structure, *the sole guilt of the God ailing of himself*, is wholly passed by, wholly eliminated and, naturally, left wholly unexploited.

For good reason: the mere mention of it would, of its own, would have overthrown the whole of Adorno's psychological edifice, since it allows Wagner to deal with psychology in the same contemptuous manner as Wotan when he "orders Hunding to go."

Of especial interest is the malevolent jargon with which Adorno attacks Wagner's text. Thus, without any respect for what actually happens, he writes: "....the age-old husband, Hunding, is sent to hell without much ado. But the contemptuous movement of the hand itself with which Wotan orders Hunding to go is once more a terrorist gesture." The terrorist gesture is what, according to wise psychological calculation, had to be *suggested* at every turn. The "hell", however, is a stroke of the brush which sketches in for us a gruesome concentration camp.

But, in fact, Wotan says to Hunding: "Go then, serf! Kneel to Fricka. Tell her that Wotan's spear has avenged what brought her shame." Then he sends him with a contemptuous flick of the hand straight to.....Valhalla to pay homage to "public opinion (Fricka)", which has defeated Wotan.

Nevertheless, Adorno's blindness to the pivot of Wagner's conception constitutes the ground for the sentence, incomprehensible without this blindness, which asserts the mysterious "knowing more" on the part of the music. This sentence forms a bridge across which the psychological claim to totality (All) moves towards its definitive dissolution into the mystical consolation, the Nothing for which Wagner is blamed with so much fuss. With music one is already in the circle of the 'chosen' since, as soon as music is interpreted, there speaks the enlightened specialist who is able to lead the common man and even the amateur who plays the piano or violin 'quite well' by the nose.

T.W.Adorno thus crosses the bridge provided by the "more-knowing music" and continues:

> "Turning over, the guide [i.e. Wagner's music, J.W.] of the Unconscious becomes the first Conscious: the first of which perception disposes and which can be used by perception for its own ends."

Imagine this plastically! The turned-over guide of the Wagnerian word or whatever might be meant by the "Unconscious", becomes the first *conscious* (music or guide?) of which perception disposes.

It is not yet fully grasped: the *conscious* music or guide is the first turned-over guide music of the Unconscious which can be used for its own ends by the perception which disposes of it.

No! With the best will in the world this is not to be unscrambled. To be prepared for all eventualities, in desperation I shall, nevertheless, add at least a perception which disposes of a turned over first conscious music or guide and can use them for its own ends.

Oof! And all this after one has carefully shoved Wagner's conscious composition into the dark room of repressions, biological complexes where the dumpling of the "unconscious", without which modern psychology would starve miserably for lack of sufficient stupidities, is prepared and cooked with convulsive effort. Who can describe the indescribable astonishment produced by the sight of this monster which makes its appearance disciplined to psychological freedom? For, naturally, the conscious music or the perception which disposes of this first conscious guide to the Unconscious is, because it is (great Gods, hear and avenge the insult to the noble art of printing) a perception to boot, which, apart from the "conscious" and "guide"!, disposes of no first *conscious* whatever...without any doubt this conscious and perception is, both with respect to Wagner and to all past, present and future, a nonsense faced with the dimensions of which even the strongest expletive collapses helplessly.

This takes place to the accompaniment of an exercise in elocution familiar to children in certain parts of Germany, one which, for a long time, already, seems to have been aimed at modern psychology. Here it is:

> If the purpose does not purpose the purpose which the purpose will purpose, then the whole purpose has no purpose and is totally purposeless.

On then with the text as it continues, without omission, after the turned-over guide:

> "Not completely without legitimacy did Wagner compare himself to the interpreter of dreams rather than to the dreamer. But only he can interpret the dream who is weak and strong enough to surrender himself to it once more and completely. Tristan knows not only the ecstatic music of dream and death,, not only the lust of the unconscious which 'no penance has yet cooled', because, *qua* unfree and unconscious lust, it is as unobtainable[30] as happiness in Schopenhauer's philosophy, and which, therefore, disguises itself as penance. The fevered parts of the third act of Tristan contain the black, harsh, jagged music that unveils rather than underlies the vision. Music, the most enchanting of all arts, learns to break the spell it casts on all its creations. Tristan's malediction upon love is more than the impotent sacrifice of ecstasy to asceticism: it is the rebellion of music against the compulsion of its own fate and it is only in the face of its total determination by the blind urge that it regains self-consciousness. It is not for nothing that the phrases in the Tristan score which follow the words 'the horrible potion' stand on the threshold of the new music: it is not for nothing that in the first canonical work of this new music, Schoenberg's quartet in F sharp minor, the words appear: 'Take love from me, give me your happiness'. They say that love and happiness are false in the world in which we live, and that all the power of love as been transformed into hatred of the world that exists. But whoever is capable of tearing such

---

30. Oh, for life's gruesome complexities! Tristan *knows* the lust of the unconscious so well, only, apparently, because it is *unconscious* and *unobtainable*. Indeed, such expertness no penance has yet cooled: cold water works miracles in such cases. For the oxy-moronic proposition that a phenomenon may both 'conscious' and 'unconscious and unobtainable' simultaneously, no explanation is offered.

metal from the waves of Wagner;'s orchestra, could, from its altered sound derive that consolation which it stubbornly refuses with ecstasy and phantasmagoria. By giving expression to the fear of helpless men, it could, in however weak and disguised manner, become a means of helping the helpless, and renew the promise made by the age old protestation uttered by music: Live without fear!"

This, at long last, is, to the very last word, the result of social research - the full sized monster, the vacuum, the nothing. One leans back exhausted; darkness falls around; quiet descends upon the battlefield. While one is still wondering whether it might not be preferable to struggle with fear against the vacuum, it appears that the world in which Adorno's false love reigns, in which even the hatred into which the broken "power" of false love has been transformed, has become impotent. Adorno has, in sum, characterised the attitude of Wagner's music as 'accompanying'. But then, music has rebelled against the compulsion of its own fate. After that, it has, as the 'conscious', been 'purposed'.But the purpose has failed and now dame music waits for one more "capable" than perception. But capable of what? Why, to tear such (?!) metal (?!) from Wagner's orchestra.

Is Schoenberg's music perhaps a consolation for those who belong to the helpless? Rather stick with Wagner:

> "If you want to please the people, I think it then but right that you should also learn from them whether this gave them pleasure."

Therewith: Goodnight and pleasant dreams.